C000121687

BARRY MARSHALL

As a rider, Barry Marshall was the first British man to be awarded the Union Jack pocket badge for dressage, representing Great Britain at various events including a World Championship. He is now an International and World Cup Dressage Judge and has also been Chef d'Equipe to the British Dressage Team several times, including the Barcelona Olympic Games. He also trains riders and horses at Advanced Level and teaches and tests judges at all grades, being a member of the Dressage Judges Committee of the British Horse Society. His experience of dressage in these varying roles has given him a wide working knowledge from which many may benefit.

This shows the rider asking for the bend with her inside leg. She has made the mistake of leaning her body to the inside.

DRESSAGE FROM ALL ANGLES

BARRY MARSHALL

J.A. ALLEN
London

British Library Cataloguing in Publication Data
A catalogue record for this book is available
from the British Library

ISBN 0.85131.661.1

Published in Great Britain in 1996 by
J.A. Allen and Company Limited,
1 Lower Grosvenor Place,
Buckingham Palace Road,
London, SW1W 0EL.

Typeset in Hong Kong by Setrite Typesetters Ltd.
Printed in Hong Kong by Dah Hua Printing Press Co. Ltd.

Designed by Nancy Lawrence
Illustrations by Maggie Raynor
Cartoons by Anne Pilgrim
Edited by Martin Diggle

Contents

Contents

Contents

List of Illustrations

Photographic Acknowledgements

Photographs by Elizabeth Furth, Bob Langrish, John Birt, Iain Burns and Paul Raper-Züllig

Cover photos
Front: Emile Faurie on Virtu
Back left: Carl Hester on Otto
Back right: Tracey Woodhead on Riverman

Acknowledgements

The FEI definitions of movements quoted within the text are reproduced with the permission of the Federation Equestre Internationale.

I also wish to acknowledge with thanks the help and support I have received from the following people:

Bill Tompkins, Miss Hardy and Margaret Eames, who gave me my start in horses.

Bob and Jean Bates, without whom I would never have got to shows in my early days.

Sue Blickslager and 'Tommy', where my teaching career began.

My Grand Prix horses, Othello and Octavia.

Domini Morgan, who encouraged me as a rider, trainer and judge.

My wife, Léonie, without whose help and encouragement I would never have achieved my international status or written this book.

Finally thanks to Liz Price, whose word processing skills made this book possible, and Martin Diggle, for his editing skills.

Introduction

This book, based upon my experience as an International rider, trainer and judge, has been written with the object of providing the three departments of the competitive dressage scene with an opportunity to relate to each other's points of view. Directives are given to judges to assist them in making their assessments, advice is offered to trainers on the presentation of their pupils and suggestions are made to riders, both to help them understand their aims and to evaluate the 'feel' of the various movements. The FEI definitions have been included so that they may be referred to easily.

PART ONE
Preliminary Thoughts

This horse appears to be going in good balance; the neck is perhaps drawn back slightly too much.

RESPONSIBILITY

The Judge

KNOWLEDGE

Being a good judge requires a great depth of knowledge acquired over many years, resulting from experience both of judging and riding the movements in all tests up to Grand Prix Level. Training a horse yourself is one of the best ways to acquire knowledge; combining what you are seeing with awareness of the 'feel' – which is the factor determining correct assessment of the cause of a problem. Knowing the *cause* of a fault allows better judgement to be made. You will know, from having found solutions yourself, which are the easier faults to correct and which, if they become established, can be most detrimental to progressive training. Some examples of the latter are:

1) A major problem can be lack of true balance for, without this, the quality of all gaits will be affected – in size and freedom of the steps, in regularity, rhythm and cadence.

2) A stiff or 'one-sided' horse will not have the ability to show any real suppleness either laterally – in half-passes, shoulder-in, etc. – or horizontally – in showing a back which is rounded and swinging under the rider.

3) Inadequate training of correct acceptance of the aids (that is to say, the co-ordinated use of seat, legs and hands) leads to many difficulties including resistance, lack of engagement and inability to collect.

Without balance, suppleness, engagement and obedience from the horse, the rider will be unable to utilise the degree of impulsion needed to acquire high marks. He will also be dependent on these factors to ride transitions with fluency and ease.

The rider's position in the saddle is crucial to his ability to use the aids correctly and to good effect.

ASSESSMENTS

Having the knowledge of the causes of problems gives the judge a chance to make acceptable assessments, but all assessments can be difficult when you have to weigh one thing against another. However, the longer you train for the job, the more 'computed' your brain will become: rather like learning to use the pedals automatically when driving a car, you will, over a period, learn to make sound assessments without consciously analysing every detail. You will become able to sift the good from the bad and, almost subconsciously, get to the root of a difficulty. Of course, being human, you will sometimes make a poor assessment, but the important thing is to do your best.

MARKING

Doing your best is a considerable strain. There is a lot of very exhausting concentration involved, which requires practice and discipline. As there are likely to be many competitors in a class, you will have to work accurately and fast, for if you dither too long over a mark you may miss the next movement! Getting the marks down is the first criterion. Giving a brief explanation for a low mark (five and below) comes next and, if time permits, a brief helpful comment is nice. At the end of the test, the collective marks must reflect the test itself. For instance, if a rider has not achieved very good marks through the test he will not warrant a good riding mark, however well known he may be! If, on the other hand, a horse has gained average marks – mostly fives and sixes – you cannot then fairly give a four to any of the end marks.

If you have given a wide range of marks throughout the test you should give careful consideration to which of the collective marks should be lowest. It is always puzzling to know what to do with the mark for paces when one of them is below par while the other two are quite good; or when the horse's obedience is impeccable through the whole test bar one movement, or when a rider's position and aids are less than good but the horse goes well in spite of this! These dilemmas are constant enemies of the judge, and give good reason to reach for the Anadin! Only experience and constant training will help you through.

THE NEED TO BE STRONG-MINDED

Probably every judge has a 'pet dislike' for one reason or another, and you may be no exception, being tempted to put the accent of your disapproval upon it. But we should all be aware of our own failings so, however strongly you feel, no bias should be allowed to creep into your judgement. Bias, moreover, can work both ways: you will be well aware that it is not easy to mark down a 'name' — one of those 'stars' who is accustomed to winning — but if this is necessary, you must not be weak-minded. After all, anyone can have a bad day!

The most important thing is to be true to yourself and not to be swayed by discussions prior to a competition or by prior knowledge of a specific horse or rider. Also, you must be strict with yourself and mark what you see, or believe you see, on the day.

DUTIES ON THE DAY

Your first duty is to arrive at the show in plenty of time! There is nothing more worrying for the organisers than if the judge is late — they will be wondering whether you will turn up — and nothing is more flustering for you than arriving at the last minute and trying to find your arena and writer.

Having reported to the secretary or organiser, find out exactly what time you start (there may have been an overnight alteration), collect your judging sheets, pens, etc. and introduce yourself to your writer. You will then need to find out which is your arena and whether you are judging from your car, someone else's, or a judges' box. Also, check which marker you will be required to sit at. If you are on your own this will, of course, be C but, if judging with others, it may be H, M, E, or B. (If you are the judge at C you are responsible for ringing the bell in the event of someone taking the wrong course.) Get into position in plenty of time and check the letters round the arena and then the test. Explain to your writer how you will be judging (whether you give your marks or comments first) and warn them of any places where marks have to be given extra quickly or out of order. For instance, in some Advanced tests, walk pirouettes are marked with the collected walk mark to be given separately. Most good writers will prompt you if you start to get behind with the marks. Ask them to do this.

Start the class on time and try to keep to the times on your starting list. It is virtually impossible to catch up if you get behind. Sometimes, organisers do not give quite long enough between tests or do not allow for someone who goes through the test too slowly. If this happens, do not panic – you may be able to make up time in the tea break.

Obviously, you must know the test which you are judging thoroughly and know exactly where the marks have to be given. They do not always come where you think, so look carefully. You must also be conversant with the rules and check mentally on the equipment of rider and horse prior to the test. Although competitors should also know the rules, they do make mistakes and it is always a shame to have to eliminate someone for leaving the horse's boots on, carrying a whip or not wearing spurs where applicable. However, do not pre-judge before a competitor starts the test. Also, try not to give the signal to start as the horse passes the bonnet of your car! As the rider comes up the centre line try to look agreeable even if you do not feel like it! It is very off-putting for the rider if you are wearing a severe expression.

Throughout the test, your concentration must be total. There will sometimes be distractions, but you must not allow your attention to wander towards some beautiful horse in the next arena or friends in the distance.

Hopefully, you will get on well with your writer. If a writer turns out to be disagreeable, do not try to talk; just get on with the job, having first done your best to put them at ease. If you get one who talks too much, either ask them politely not to or give them so much to do that it keeps them quiet!

Throughout your evaluation of the test, try to be as positive as you can; look for attributes to mark up rather than the opposite. The faults will strike you quickly enough; good points are sometimes harder to find. Remember that you are responsible to the worst in the class as well as the best. It is not satisfactory to put down those who are going less well without having even evaluated them against each other. Most competitors have worked hard and spent a lot of money to get to a show, and are worthy of fair judgement. However experienced you are, it is far more difficult to judge a poor test than a good one, so even more effort is needed to come up with a fair result.

At the end of the test, do check that all the marks are where they should be. Try to have a quick look to see if your writer's comments are legible and appropriate to the mark. Check that loss of points for wrong course, use of voice, etc. are registered and sign the sheet with a clear signature.

During the class there may be a short break. Do avoid looking at the scoreboard. It can be very distracting to find that you are not agreeing at all with a co-judge or that the marks are not coming out as you expected. This is just too bad. Everyone is entitled to their opinion and competitors have to learn to accept that fact.

After the class you will need to return your judge's board and pens to the secretary. Do make sure that there are no stray mark sheets lurking in your car before you go home. In any event, you should remain long enough to look at the results, or in case you are needed to clarify any points connected with your class.

As a judge you are there to judge, but do not miss any opportunities to watch other classes, sit in with more experienced judges or glean information from observing competitors riding-in. All this sort of thing is very interesting and can be of use to you. Over the course of time you may become well acquainted with many of the competitors. Although you may even be close friends with some, it is perhaps wise to distance yourself from everyone prior to judging. It is only too easy to be caught in the trap of wishing to be kind to someone and overdoing it, being affected by something said in conversation, or simply being remarked upon by those who do not know you as biased in so-and-so's favour!

After the class you may well wish to distance yourself when the results come up but, if you are confident that your judgement is honest, you should not fear anyone's attitude, nor their questions — so long as they are asked for the right reasons. Some competitors can be unreasonable or even launch an attack on your judgement. They probably do this from disappointment or lack of knowledge. Although you may not have got it right, you have given up your time so that the competition can take place so, if criticisms are levelled at you, they should be dealt with sympathetically but firmly! Being a judge is a thankless task and very hard work. You must really *want* to do the job, be able to give the time, and be prepared to devote a considerable amount of energy to studying the subject.

Lastly, when you receive an invitation to judge do reply as quickly as possible. If you accept, do arrive at the show on the right day! Also, I believe it is important to be as smartly attired as you can.

You may wish to distance yourself when the results come up.

RESPONSIBILITY

The Trainer

You have many duties as a trainer: to rider and horse; sometimes to owners or other individuals involved when working with a team; to your country if producing an international rider, but, most of all, to yourself and your sport. For one reason or another it is not always easy to follow your beliefs, but it is important to try not to be persuaded by other influences in directions you do not wish to go. This is not to say that, however experienced you are, you should shut your mind. This would be disastrous, as the more you know, the more you need to know and the easier it is to learn – for learn you should until you are no longer doing the job. It is surprising who you can learn from! I have found that all sorts of interesting details crop up in the most unlikely places, and it is never wise to write off anyone as uninteresting or of no importance.

To deal with temperaments, both equine and human, you will need to be something of a psychoanalyst. In order to make progress, your students must be receptive but, as with all of us, their state of mind is often determined by factors totally unrelated to riding. Mental distraction frequently affects the way we ride and, however much effort it takes, it will fall on you to develop your own method of gaining your pupils' concentration.

Some days it will also be hard for you, especially if you feel unwell or have your own distractions and worries. Only when you have learned to cover them up, presenting a good front and bringing your mind to the job in hand, will you be a true professional.

One of the most important points to accept when teaching is that, first and foremost, you are responsible for your pupils' safety. It is your job to see possible dangers and reduce risks. Ultimately it is the rider who accepts the main risk but, nevertheless, your initial assessment of pupil, horse, tack and schooling area should be made. Surfaces can be unsuitable or slippery; there may be some dangerous object lying about; tack may need repair; stirrups may be too small, or the horse may be badly bitted or in some unsatisfactory gadget. There are many things to look for but, so long as you are aware, you will be able to avert many, if not all, dangers.

Naturally, your main job is to impart knowledge gained from your own experience. If you have been a successful competitor, riding tests at all levels and training a variety of horses, you will have a good foundation upon which to work. You will know the 'feel' of the exercise you have to teach. You will know how to approach each exercise and the work that has to be done as preparation. You will understand the process of mental and physical build up and you will not ask your pupils to attempt any exercise before they are capable. When things go wrong, you will know that a return to basics is required. Also, you will try to build a solid base, working on your pupils' positions and use of aids whilst helping them to establish all basic necessities for their horses' progress.

Teaching people and training horses can be a hard, tedious business, but if you really put yourself into it, it can provide a lot of job satisfaction. So much rests upon the desires of riders to achieve success and upon the aptitude of both horse and rider. Without a pupil's basic ability and devout intention to work hard, your efforts will be to no avail.

If you are a conscientious teacher, you will give much of yourself in effort. It is not enough to simply stand and shout directions. Much thought as to the best approach, decisions over which exercises would be most beneficial on that day, use of your own technique drawn from a wide experience, plus a capacity to use initiative – sometimes even deviousness – to arrive at your goal is called for. Your horizon may vary from pupil to pupil, as some will progress more slowly than others but, in my opinion, you should always *aim* for the top. You should not give any less to those who say they aim for less because, with sufficient dedication, almost anyone can get to Grand Prix standard.

There will always be those who fall halfway up the mountain but, with the grit and determination that you can help to give them, some will make it to the summit. If you are a person with very high standards yourself, this will rub off on your pupils. They will need to be driven; gently at first then harder as time goes on. It will also be up to them to take what they want from you, and you should be prepared to answer their queries in a way which makes everything as logical as possible. If your knowledge of cause and effect is thorough, then your explanations will be clear and make complete sense; there will be no mystery about the training, which will be perfectly comprehensible.

High standards demand much effort. Your piloting will take your pupils through both calm and stormy waters but, by clever navigation, you can make the way as smooth as possible. During difficult times you will be required to provide all the encouragement possible, giving your pupils confidence in their progress so that they do not feel inadequate and falter, but are driven on by inspiration and enthusiasm.

Rapport between horse and rider, rider and teacher is a necessity for success. You may find that you just cannot get on with some people, nor they with you but, in all teaching, I believe you should keep a sense of proportion and essentially a sense of humour. There are many individuals who, though serious students, respond best to a light approach, whereas others prefer a sterner attitude.

It is important, I think, to teach your pupils to accept that small improvements are worthwhile. This is not always easy, especially with riders who have high ideals themselves. Such people may drive themselves and their horses too far, too soon and it is you who have to 'put the brakes on' for them. On the whole, though, you will be the one pushing for new work, which is very necessary, as I do think that some trainers leave their pupils in the lower stages too long.

Training horses is hard work but it can be very satisfying. Teaching people to train horses can be soul-destroying. The main thing is to care about horses and their way of going. If you do care enough, this will help you through the many frustrations which occur. As one of your main jobs will probably be producing pupils for competition, you will need to be familiar with all rules and requirements at the different levels. For instance, the degree of collection called for in Elementary will necessarily be less than in Medium, and so on. You should be aware of how marks are distributed in tests and where the accent is placed, if you are to help your pupils win. For example, if one movement involves a half-pass in trot followed by a transition to canter, the half-pass should have greater emphasis than the transition. In short, you need to be able to judge yourself – if not officially, at least to see things from a judge's point of view.

Teaching, of course, requires full understanding in the teacher, as does helping riders to compromise the 'feel' in the arena. No-one wants to accept less than the best but, for one reason or another, it is not always possible to obtain it and, rather than become agitated, riders must learn that sometimes mistakes and faults have to be covered up or disguised in order to get through a test. Forgetting the test is very distracting, but you can help your pupils by teaching them to learn a pattern if there is one, to repeat exercises frequently and to be able, if they *do* forget, to begin again confidently. Also, you have to be able to help riders with problems of temperament; those who become over-anxious and tense, as well as those who cannot raise their adrenalin level to that needed to 'attack' a test.

Teaching *flair* is almost impossible. It is generally either in a rider or not. With sound training it at least becomes possible for a rider to go into the arena with great determination and to 'ride for their life!' A high degree of accuracy and clear definition of movements should be a priority of training, particularly as pupils progress towards Grand Prix. Even if they do not, many more marks are within grasp if attention is given to detail. You should always be prepared to study judges' sheets with pupils, to give explanations or discuss anything confusing.

You should be aware of the fact that no judge is able to give marks for potential, neither is he gifted with insight into past work, so he is unable to give praise for improvements which you see and which your pupil may feel. Disappointment may occur when the rider knows of the improvement, but is not rewarded by the marks. You will be able to explain the job of a judge – that he can only mark what he sees on the day, and that if he has not recognised progress of which you are both aware he should not be blamed. You will almost certainly disagree with judges from time to time, and be frustrated by a few who lack the ability to really see what is going on. Unfortunately, there are as few gifted judges as there are riders and trainers, so the poor aptitude of some is hardly surprising.

It can be hard trying to stick to your principles of training if they are not recognised by others, but this is all part of the job. You will soon learn to tell your pupils who to avoid or who to go under. Basically, however, try not to allow prejudice to colour your instruction, as this can encourage negative thinking from pupils, who find it easier to blame the judge than themselves for poor marks!

It is all too easy to become 'stable blind', that is to say, believing that the animals and pupils under your instruction are the best. A good trainer puts a lot of himself into students who, if successful, will naturally stand out in his eyes. It is essential to be critical of yourself, with methods constantly under review, and when pupils return from a show with their judging sheets, try to see the comments through the judges' eyes. They will not have been made lightly and however unlikely they may appear there is usually a grain of truth there somewhere. Although it is important to have the courage of your convictions it is sometimes necessary to admit to yourself that you may have been wrong.

Your teaching should be based upon the classical trainers; experts who have proved their worth in past years, many of whom have written books or competed themselves. Being open-minded and constantly studying, you will develop your own way of bringing pupils to a high standard. To be successful, you will have to introduce points from many sources, including the most highly acclaimed teachings of the countries whose riders attain Olympic medals. European influence is high on this list – in particular the German school, which has a strong record of producing winners.

Training horses and riders at all levels puts great demands on you, not only on your knowledge but also your versatility in coping with an enormous variety of problems. It is this constant challenge, plus a strong determination to win which will motivate you but, to these qualities, you will need to add resilience and resolution.

RESPONSIBILITY

The Rider

Riding is all about 'feel'. You may have this naturally or you may have to be taught it, but either way it is your main asset.

Your responsibilities as a rider are twofold; to your horse and to yourself.

DUTY TO THE HORSE

Your first responsibility is to your horse, whose welfare and mental and physical development are totally in your control. If his development is worked on patiently and diligently, this will pay dividends. If worked at intermittently, or rushed, the result will be a poor base upon which little can be built. Each horse should be treated as an individual; his character discovered, his learning capacity assessed, his ability for the various exercises established. His co-operation will depend upon your understanding and consistency. The horse can only progress through clear explanations and suitable praise (a pat on the neck is adequate).

'Know where you are going and in which gear' is not a bad maxim to follow! Ensure that you prepare your horse adequately for what you want to do, so that he is in a position to comply. A primary objective of dressage is to enhance and beautify the horse's natural gaits and appearance by developing him physically, so that he is correctly muscled and suppled like an athlete, and can work with the grace, energy and precision of a gymnast. There is nothing more heartbreaking than to see a beautiful horse with lovely gaits being destroyed by thought-less, ignorant riding, nor anything so distressing as a horse made confused and anxious through the muddled thinking of his rider.

We all hope to attain great heights, and aiming for the top is the right thing to do — so long as we know what our responsi-bilities are, grasp them firmly and climb steadily up the ladder. There will be the occasional slip or step backwards, but deter-mination can overcome all difficulties.

DUTY TO YOURSELF

Your duty to yourself is to maximise your chance of success by learning as much as you possibly can. This learning comes in a variety of ways. It is very instructive to watch others — especially experts of all nationalities — not only in competition but, if you get the chance, training at their homes, or riding-in at shows. Much can be gleaned from close observation. While experts will give you an idea of what is right, a lot can also be learned by watching less knowledgeable riders, seeing what looks wrong and seeking to find an answer within your own experi-ence. Watching others ride tests is invaluable. Mistakes in accuracy, definition of movements, preparation and presen-tation are only too painfully obvious from the ground, but give essential insight into what the judge will see. Videos can be well worth watching, especially those of yourself! These often

Videos of yourself can give unpleasant shocks.

15

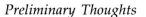

give unpleasant shocks, but can tell you a lot about the result of your riding! You will become more aware of faults as your knowledge increases, and this will only happen if you keep an open mind.

It is important that you never become blind to deficiencies in your own or your horse's ability and that you should be self-critical and modest, accepting advice and tuition from those more experienced than yourself. You will have much to study. Books are necessary to your acquisition of knowledge, either to discover something new or as a check on work you have attempted. To know your subject in depth will take many years, with much practical experience together with the study of the works of the Masters of classical dressage. Riding in competition will mean also studying judges' mark sheets. This can sometimes be rather unpleasant, as you have to see yourself as others see you, but their comments must be looked into and their value and relevance to your performance assessed.

A good trainer will be able to help you to understand what judges are looking for, what their priorities are in a particular movement and the reasoning behind a criticism. He should help you to overcome disappointment and feelings of despair. You and the trainer should work together towards producing the picture that the judge wants to see. Beware of the pitfall of believing you are right and the judge is wrong. Judges do go through much rigorous training themselves and will be trying to do their best. They will be wrong sometimes, that is unavoidable, but you must accept that you can be wrong too!

Only by dedication and sheer hard work can you hope to gain rewards. This means riding every day, evaluating your schooling session and deliberating upon the plan for the next day. Never ride without a clear idea of what you are aiming for and, most important, try to find out what causes your horse to react in certain ways, and what effect this has on his way of going. Only then can you anticipate an outcome and know how to prevent many mistakes from occurring.

Criticism is never easy to accept, but is inevitable from time to time. Try to look at it honestly and do not put the blame on the horse, your trainer or the judge. If you do, you will only be cheating yourself. If you can look at your own work, relating it to an ultimate image in your mind, and be truthful to yourself, you should arrive one day at your goal.

CHOICE OF HORSE
The Judge

This subject is not, of course, really relevant to the judge, who cannot choose the horses he judges. However, all of us tend to have a type of horse we prefer to watch and we may also veer towards preference of a particular type of action. This is human nature and is inevitable. The reason I mention it is to point out the possible pitfall of marking up something you like to see. Your mental image of how you want to see a dressage horse going should be consistent. The variation of type and action superimposed upon the image requires fair-mindedness on your part, with any prejudice pushed into the background. It is not always easy to divorce yourself from preferring the beautiful to the plain; the Thoroughbred to the commoner; flowing action to a more heavy-footed action — or perhaps you just cannot see why everyone does not ride a warmblood! Of course, there are good and bad points in everything but, so far as you are concerned, your job is to see past the facade into the training beyond. One word about markings. Horses with white on their legs can sometimes give an optical illusion as to levelness of stride. Beware of being taken in or influenced by anyone else's suggestions — make up your own mind!

CHOICE OF HORSE

The Trainer

There will probably be occasions when you are asked to find a horse for a client, at which juncture I believe there are certain points to take into account. The governing one will most likely be finance, so this will inevitably dictate what you can find that is suitable for the price. You will very probably have taught your client for some time, so will have a pretty good idea of their capability. It is obviously pointless to recommend a horse to them, however right for the job, if you know that they will not be able to ride him! You will be aware of whether a young horse, or one who has been around a bit, would be right for them; whether they want to or can train a horse themselves, or whether a schoolmaster would be a better idea.

Whatever horse you decide is right, they have also got to like him. Persuading people to buy on your say-so never really works unless they also feel happy about it. Having found a horse with the right conformation, action, age and temperament, of a height that will suit your pupil, go and try him, preferably before taking your pupil along. You can then avoid wasting your time and everyone else's if, when you get there, you spot a stable vice or the horse shows an unlevelness or faulty action, or gives an unsatisfactory ride.

CONFORMATION

There are certain points of conformation which I believe are very important. I think that the horse should have a naturally rounded outline, that is to say, rounded hindquarters which are built with the hind legs underneath them, not out behind. The tail should not be set on too low, as this gives the quarters a crouching look about them.

The length of back should be such that the saddle sits well back from the shoulders, but does not show excessive space between the back of the saddle and the loins. The neck should rise from the withers into an arched crest, with a good line on the underneck and no thickness where it joins the head.

The head itself should be proportional to the body; a heavy head is usually ugly. The ears should not be too big nor 'lop', as this spoils the picture of the topline.

The horse's body should not be top-heavy for the amount of bone he has, nor show too much 'daylight'. The amount of bone will naturally depend on the type of horse, but very heavy limbs or fragile ones usually look unattractive.

ACTION

You will probably have your own preferences regarding action, but there are some things to avoid and others to accept. I think that the most acceptable action is a straight mover (seen from in front or behind). Plaiting is undesirable — it can be quite horrendous seen from the front! Dishing can be a problem if too exaggerated but, in a minor form, is not of importance.

The horse should also show plenty of natural flexion of the joints. This gives an impression of activity, which is very helpful to the overall picture. I have found that horses with limited joint flexion are marked less well in tests as, although they may actually be working quite hard, they do not look to be doing so!

After careful consideration of all the details, a decision to advise purchase can be made. This is a big responsibility, so you must be very certain about your choice. Finally, it is also your job to advise your client to have the horse inspected by a veterinary surgeon for soundness, as this is an area which you cannot be expected to cover.

CHOICE OF HORSE

The Rider

Although choice is always difficult, it is nicer to have a horse of your own choosing rather than one foisted upon you by someone else. No doubt you will have a picture in your mind of the type of horse you fancy; the colour, how you want him to move, and so on. I have a very clear picture of the horse I would choose but have found, over the years, that I have ended up with something of totally different colour or type, simply because one has come along with the right ability. All I am suggesting is that you have no preconceived ideas from which you refuse to budge! Keep an open mind and view all prospects with thoughts as to movement, temperament and a pleasing picture.

Because there are so many types to choose from, it may be hard to decide, but the important thing is that the horse suits you. Thoroughbreds can look most appealing, but you do need to be of calm and patient disposition to ride one, as they can be easily upset or excited. A great big upstanding warmblood may 'look the goods', but if you are short and dumpy you will never ride him satisfactorily. Certainly, try to look for a horse whose height suits you. Just because everyone else appears to be riding 16.2s does not mean that you need to do the same — some of our best horses have only been 15.2 hh.

Naturally, we would all like a horse with perfect conformation. Such horses can generally operate properly because they are constructed in the right way. Having said that, I have also known many who I would not have looked at twice standing

20

If you are short and dumpy, a big warmblood will not suit you.

still, but who looked exceedingly impressive on the move. Movement is all-important. Active, expressive gaits with an air of 'look at me' are what you should be seeking.

Regarding conformation, a pretty head is not essential, but a naturally arched crest is. Although work will build a neck up, it must be the right shape to start with. If it grows out of the shoulders from below the wither, you will never be able to bring it into the right outline. A long back can be a hindrance from the point of view of engaging the hindquarters. Naturally active hind legs built under the quarters are a great advantage. Straight action, though preferable, is not essential but a horse who moves without much flexion of his joints will never look quite so active as one who does.

Always see a horse loose in a school before you buy him, so that you can see his natural scope, and always see him ridden before you ride him. Many an accident has resulted from a rider getting on a strange horse without seeing the owner riding first. Do not accept any excuses either – these are a sure sign that he might be dodgy!

THE RIDER

The Judge

The rider mark given at the end of a test should reflect the rider's ability, not only in respect of having given correct aids, but in having given them in such a way that they were effective.

How good a rider looks, or however well known he may be, if the horse fails to perform a movement or movements, the rider should be held accountable. Therefore it would not be right to give a high mark if the marks for the movements were moderate or worse. Conversely, if marks throughout the test were high, the rider mark should match.

A correct position in the saddle, if sustained and combined with effective aids, should influence the horse's way of going to advantage. If this position is not sustained, if it shows insecurity or dependence on the reins, its influence cannot be satisfactory. The mark given should take this into account.

Dressage is, of course, about correct training, but part of this is to produce a pleasing picture. Each of us will need to evaluate in our own way what this is. Occasionally, a rider who has a natural gift for 'feel', but does not have a classical position, will come along to confound all the rules! In this case, you should try to assess them from the result they obtained from the horse which, if successful, would mean a slight deviation from the normal train of thought.

Sometimes, especially at the lower levels, you may wish to comment on some aspect of a person's riding. Although you are there to judge, not to teach, a brief, helpful suggestion may be welcome – and should, I believe, be made for the horse's sake.

THE RIDER

The Trainer

Quite clearly, one of your main tasks is to teach your pupils how to sit correctly and how to apply the aids. The classical position was evolved by the great Masters because it gave the rider the best chance to influence the horse correctly and achieve the best way of going. Similarly, the aids were devised as the most effective method of communication. Their consistent use, combined with a secure position in the saddle, provides the rider and horse with the maximum opportunity for success. To deviate from proven methods is unwise for, however talented a rider is, he may not be able to find a good enough alternative. Your job, I believe, is to assist the rider to follow the proven methods and work to perfect them.

Security of position can probably be best achieved by riding without stirrups. At some stage, a lunge horse could provide the opportunity to consolidate this work by allowing the rider the chance to ride without reins or stirrups. Only when the seat has become deep enough will the rider find the capacity to use the aids to maximum effect.

The effect of the aids will be shown in the horse's response to them. If there is insufficient response, your job should be to teach the rider how to be more positive without becoming untidy or rough. This is where your own technique and knowledge will be tested. Some riders are naturally passive while others tend to be overactive, or have the effect of making horses 'hot up'. You should be capable of dealing with all such problems and be able to bring horse and rider into unity.

THE RIDER

The Rider

When you take your first riding lesson you will be taught how to sit on the horse and will learn to use a basic set of aids. If you are taught correctly this basis will not change, although it will be developed and enlarged to become more sophisticated.

Your aim should be to establish yourself in a classical position on the horse; one which not only holds you securely, but also promotes your ability to absorb the horse's movement and become part of a harmonious entity. The communication system – the aids – should, if used correctly, provide you with the opportunity to work together. If you fail to develop the right technique, instead of unity taking you up the ladder there will be opposition, which can only hold you back.

Sitting well on your horse and 'looking the part' is important, but unless you are an effective rider, able to make a horse do what you want, you will not get far. Learning to use your aids positively and yet sympathetically takes patience and hard work.

You will need endurance and determination – riding tests is extremely hard work. It may look easy, but every detail is crucial, since you should aim to be in control of every step taken. Any faults will be yours and yours alone. Your horse is your 'instrument' – it is up to you how you play him!

PART TWO
Expectations

It is always nice to see the horse rewarded for his effort.

PRELIMINARY AND NOVICE LEVELS

The Judge

At this standard, a judge would like to see controlled freedom. If this sounds like a contradiction, I should explain that it refers to the natural stride and desire of the horse to go forwards, controlled in such a way that freedom is allowed within the confines of the required movements. The preservation of the correct gaits should be paramount. The attitude of the horse towards his work is also very important.

Crookedness, resistance or irregularities, lack of rhythm and balance, stiffness or hollowing are all faults which, if seen at this stage, could prevent progress, and affect the horse's future. These faults should definitely be penalised while, in the rider mark, direction may be given towards correcting a problem that may be hampering the outcome.

The level of impulsion at this stage should be sufficient for the horse to perform all the movements required without labouring. He should show activity and be going in a rounded outline, but should never be on the forehand. In the past, the old expression 'long and low' has often been the cause of a lack of impulsion and balance, with horses being allowed to flop along without energy and without being 'on the aids'. Naturally, collection is not expected at this time, but a judge should certainly want to see in this groundwork the correct basis upon which to build future work.

If the outline and impulsion appear more advanced than one might expect then, provided that the horse is working well, the judge should be overjoyed! Many good horses are spoilt and their future destroyed by incorrect training. It is important to reward those who show the ingredients that could take them to Grand Prix.

A pleasing, willing expression.

PRELIMINARY AND NOVICE LEVELS

The Trainer

This is the time when you will be required to lay down the rules for all the future work. So far as the horse is concerned, he will need to learn to respect his rider, to begin the process of understanding and to start the physical development needed.

You have to produce correct gaits which are balanced and rhythmic, in which the horse can operate without stress or strain. Knowledge of the exercises used to bring this about is essential as is the ability to advise the rider how to engage the horse effectively to provide adequate activity and energy.

The rider may also need help and guidance on many other aspects of the work, as well as being corrected as necessary on position and use of aids.

As this level is the key to the future of both horse and rider, it should be attended to with the greatest care, each step of the way being constantly checked for flaws. Only a trainer who is devoted to producing horses in the right way can do this. Correct gaits are essential and anything that goes wrong at this basic stage may never be eradicated.

Although riders may have a limited view of their capabilities, you will want to push them to that limit and, if possible, beyond. Energy and willpower are needed to provide the necessary motivation as you must drive yourself as well as your pupil. Good dressage trainers have this ability, with obvious benefits. This level is an exciting one. In your mind's eye you will hold a picture of the horse at Grand Prix level. If you can see potential you have the chance to shape it to that end.

PRELIMINARY AND NOVICE LEVELS

The Rider

Your chief task at this time is to be aware of the correct balance in which your horse has to be working in order to perform the movements you want to ride.

Novice horses do not need to be allowed to work on the forehand. In fact, you must try to focus your attention on transferring weight onto the hindquarters as early as you can. This does not mean that the horse has to be collected – gathered together, yes, but in no way restricted or constrained.

When you go in for your first test, the judge will want to see good activity in the gaits and sufficient impulsion to enable you to perform the movements with ease. Obtaining the latter is dependent on each individual horse. There are no rules; you have to regulate energy to balance, being able to build it up or reduce it in order to facilitate manouvreability.

A steady outline is vital to getting good marks. This should not feel fixed by the aids, especially the hands, but must be brought about by having the hindquarters engaged; the horse working actively with a supple back and yielding mouth.

In your daily work, make sure that you never neglect straightness (hind legs following the forelegs) and that you pay particular attention to regular steps in a consistent rhythm.

Your aim should be to progress towards higher tests, not to become stuck at this level. Although it is essential to have the basics right it is also important mentally and physically to move on. Knowledge of school exercises and how they should be ridden will help you towards this end.

ELEMENTARY AND MEDIUM LEVELS

The Judge

The horse should be showing definite signs that he is moving towards Advanced Level.

Impulsion and activity should now be increased, with greater emphasis on the power of the hindquarters to 'carry' the horse. Self-carriage should thus be more established, the horse remaining in an outline approaching the ultimate.

Regularity and correct sequence of gaits should be uppermost in the mind during the assessment of movements. Distinct differences of gait should now be possible, with direct and accurate transitions. All variations should be obvious; the extensions, while not yet at their maximum, should still display a positive difference from medium movements.

All the work should be showing greater precision, but should still be free and unconstrained. Obedience and submission ought now to be good, with consequently low incidence of evasion and resistance.

The rider's position and use of aids should be such that the performance appears light and easy.

Allowances are, of course, made at this standard for the fact that it is a transitional stage between Novice and Advanced. Some horses will tend towards the lower level, while others will show higher quality work. Assessments should draw attention to those problems which could restrict or prevent further progress.

Many good horses are 'lost' at this stage, never to go any further. Judges do bear a responsibility to acknowledge those who are heading in the right direction despite mistakes, and to point out clearly, to those who are floundering, where their errors lie.

A very good outline.

ELEMENTARY AND MEDIUM LEVELS

The Trainer

Progression from a novice balance and outline should now have taken place. Gradual transference of weight towards the hindquarters should now enable the horse to 'carry himself' without so much help from the rider. The half-halt can be used to a greater extent for this purpose, and to bring about the required degree of collection.

Suppling exercises will give more pliability to the work and will help to overcome resistances caused by tension and stiffness.

Once self-carriage and flexibility allow, more impulsion and activity can be requested, in order to give more expression to the performance.

Provided that transitions are free from resistance, the greater power now incorporated into the gaits will enable the medium and extended movements to develop. These should begin to be clear, and sustainable over the required distances. Control over the energy facilitated by good submission and suppleness will give the steps a consistent rhythm that takes the horse through a test without faltering.

The rider's position should be secure, with independent seat permitting the application of aids that produce what is needed effectively. The rider should know how to overcome all the problems relating to the work at these Levels, being aware of faults and able to make corrections. His control should provide the ability to ride accurately without ever restricting the horse's freedom and scope.

ELEMENTARY AND MEDIUM LEVELS

The Rider

The first essential is exact knowledge of the required movements; what they are and how they should be ridden.

Watching others is very helpful and, although there will be enormous variation, a clearer picture may evolve from observation – particularly seeing how experts deal with problems. Watch carefully how top riders prepare for movements to give their horses the best possible chance. Look to see the degree of collection and extension rewarded by high marks. This will help you to make your own assessment.

At this standard, the horse should be leaving behind all those problems of loss of balance and rhythm, crookedness and stiffness. He should be accepting aids willingly while still moving freely, his work uninhibited by restriction.

Your position in the saddle should provide sufficient security so that your arms and hands can 'belong to the horse', working independently from your seat.

Ensure that at all times you retain the correct gaits; that the horse learns to stay in a round outline, and that all movements are connected by smooth, fluid transitions.

So often a good horse or rider is 'lost' after this level because they have failed to really understand collection, and instead of arriving into advanced classes with a chance of success, everything looks rigid or restricted. Make a study of the subject; discover how to engage the hindquarters adequately so that the forehand is 'carried' by the horse, not by you! Correctly ridden half-halts and shoulder-in will help you to this end.

34

ADVANCED LEVEL

The Judge

All the previous work at the different Levels should now have brought the horse to an established way of going, uninterrupted by stiffness, crookedness or resistance.

The muscles of the hindquarters should be developed and strengthened so that they can support the weight. They should be able to provide the power necessary for all the movements and be consistently active and capable of lowering.

Gaits should have developed in regularity and rhythm, so that each step is clearly defined by spring and cadence. All gait variations should be connected by fluent transitions that show a high degree of elasticity and accuracy.

Submission by the horse to his rider's demands should give the control exact precision. This can only be brought about by suppleness and freedom of stride guided by clear, effective and sympathetic aids.

The outline should always be rounded, with the poll at the highest point, arriving in that position as the result of impulsion.

A good test is one of maximum power, controlled so skilfully by the rider that it seems he is doing very little to achieve it.

The rider's position should give an impression of elegance and not be spoilt by unsightly movement of the seat or body. The hands should control the horse as if playing an instrument while any leg movement should be minimal. The horse should look easy to ride and if the aids are given correctly the horse's response will reflect this. No rider deserves a good mark if only obtaining a moderate performance from the horse.

ADVANCED LEVEL

The Trainer

This is the culmination of the building up of controlled energy. If the systematic process has been effective, the horse's physique will have been enhanced by muscular development, giving him an overall look of immense power. This strength should enable him to carry himself and his rider in excellent balance and harmony, flowing easily from one movement to another.

If the control has been gained by sensitivity on the part of the rider, from aids given sympathetically but with firmness, the horse should show no resentment of anything he may be asked. His obedience to his rider should then be given willingly — not as a result of unnecessary coercion.

The pupil should be capable of presenting the horse for each movement in such a way that the response made is to the best of the horse's ability. Pupils must have a complete understanding of how all exercises should be executed and put together, know the faults that can be expected to lose marks and have the capability to correct or cover up. Experience should have given control over nerves so that, while in the arena, full concentration can be given to achieving the best test possible. When things go wrong, a cool attitude is vital to achieving recovery. Also, a good pupil will always listen to any advice given following each test.

You, the trainer, will need to know as much or more than each rider and judge. You must be able to view the performance objectively and see it from a judge's point of view. Mistakes are very costly and, although we all want to see something that exhilarates and inspires, if these moments are interspersed with faults – however small – the overall result will be affected.

Both horse and rider present a confident picture.

ADVANCED LEVEL

The Rider

By now, you and your horse should have formed a real partnership, not only of trust, but of knowledge of each other's moods and responses to certain situations. Communication is the lifeline and, by this stage of training, you will have developed your own system, which you apply automatically and which the horse understands.

Your basic position in the saddle and the aids you use are set as a guide but, like all guides, they are not rigid. Within the framework, you and your horse can make your own arrangements – provided the results gain good marks. If they do not, it is pointless to be stubborn. Always be prepared to review your ideas and make changes if necessary. Sometimes, this can be very hard – especially if you have spent years producing a Grand Prix horse only to find that something needs quite dramatic alteration. This, of course, is why it is so important to get all ingredients in the right proportion, lest the product you thought so well produced and artistic should 'flop in the middle' in the finale.

Knowing how a judge thinks and understanding his position is very important to your own success. Be clear in your mind (and willing to accept) that, from where the judge sits, he can see things which you may barely be aware of in the effort of riding the test. At this level, even small faults can lose a lot of marks.

Judges are not trying to compare you with other horses in the class; they are endeavouring to mark against their mental picture of an ideal dressage performance. Sometimes, being human, they may get it wrong but, however tempting it may be to do so, it is unfair to blame them unduly. Judging is an exceedingly tricky and exhausting business, requiring knowledge acquired over a great length of time. Without judges who are willing to give their time and skill, there would be no opportunity for your to win competitions and attain glory. They should be respected, and attention paid to their remarks. They may be of help!

Judging dressage is an exhausting business.

Nothing but experience will enable you to decide whether you are only in a position to ride a 'safe clear' or whether you can throw caution to the wind and really 'ride for it!' I think it must be said that the majority of medals are won by the latter approach, but you need to be temperamentally cool and mentally confident, so that by 'giving your all', the judges, sitting on the edge of their seats, will feel compelled to give high marks!

A well-balanced canter with the rider sitting deep.

PART THREE
The Basic Gaits

A good medium walk.

THE WALK

The Judge

You should be thoroughly conversant with the following FEI definitions of the walk and its variants:

> 1) The walk is a marching pace in which the footfalls of the horse's feet follow one another in 'four-time', well marked and maintained in all work at the walk.
>
> 2) When the foreleg and the hind leg on the same side move almost on the same beat the walk tends to become an almost lateral movement. This irregularity, which might become an ambling movement, is a serious deterioration of the pace.
>
> 3) It is at the pace of walk that the imperfections of dressage are most evident. This is also the reason why a horse should not be asked to walk 'on the bit' at the early stages of his training. A too precipitous collection will not only spoil the collected walk, but the medium and the extended walk as well.
>
> 4) The following walks are recognised: collected walk, medium walk, extended walk, and free walk.
>
> a) **Collected walk**. The horse remaining 'on the bit' moves resolutely forward, with his neck raised and arched. The head approaches the vertical position, the light contact with the mouth being maintained. The hind legs are engaged with good hock action. The pace should remain marching and vigorous, the feet being placed in regular sequence. Each step covers less ground and is higher than at the medium walk, because all the joints bend more markedly, showing clear self-carriage. In order not to become hurried or irregular, the collected walk is shorter than the medium walk, although showing greater activity.

43

b) **Medium walk**. A free, regular and unconstrained walk of moderate extension. The horse, remaining 'on the bit', walks energetically, but calmly, with even and determined steps, the hind feet touching the ground in front of the footprints of the forefeet. The rider maintains a light, soft and steady contact with the mouth.

c) **Extended walk**. The horse covers as much ground as possible, without haste and without losing the regularity of his steps, the hind feet touching the ground clearly in front of the footprints of the forefeet. The rider allows the horse to stretch out his head and neck without, however, losing contact with the mouth.

d) **Free walk**. The free walk is a pace of relaxation in which the horse is allowed complete freedom to lower and stretch out his head and neck.

As with all the gaits, one of your duties is to observe and penalise any serious imperfections. In a test, you may not easily be able to determine what is a particular horse's natural stride, but you will be able to assess whether he overtracks satisfactorily in the medium and extended movements. You must always look first to see if the four-beat sequence of the steps is correct, especially when it comes to collection, where it often goes wrong, becoming two-beat ('pacing'). Also, the hind feet must follow in the tracks of the forefeet.

Next and most importantly, the steps must be equal in size; each hind leg taking exactly the same length of step as its partner. The joints also must flex equally, so that there is no 'hitching' upwards of a particular leg.

You will be especially concerned with the differences in the various walks. Knowing the requirements laid down in the rules should assist you very much with your assessment. Horses who have the ability to conform to the rules are easy to judge; it is those who have problems which give you a headache! For instance, how do you mark the horse who merely 'shortens his neck' instead of really collecting? Or the one who goes in irregular fashion; alters his rhythm; 'paces'; breaks gait several times; hollows his outline; does not lengthen the frame; falls onto the forehand; overbends in the free walk, and so on!

It is not possible to say that a four should be given for this fault or a three for that. So much depends on what happens either side of the fault, whether it is persistent, or how it affects the movement asked for. All I can say is that, knowing the requirement and with the purity of the gait uppermost in your mind, you must decide how much the fault occurring may affect future work, as well as the movement being performed at the time. Some faults, especially those such as irregularity, unlevelness, lack of freedom, poor outline, resistance, and incorrect collection will definitely affect future work. The occasional 'break', 'trip', loss of rhythm or momentary change in outline may be viewed less seriously in the lower tests.

Riders can be quite clever at hiding how badly their horses walk.

Some horses will have unsatisfactory walks, and their riders may be quite clever at hiding how bad they are. Clever riding can pick up marks, but do not be deceived into giving higher marks than you should.

THE WALK

The Trainer

As a trainer, you will be responsible for the most important basic factor – the correctness and purity of the gaits – so your knowledge of the sequence of steps and how to improve their quality should be uppermost in your mind. Your own knowledge of dealing with problems which arise will develop from riding many horses, and from teaching. You will discover the mistakes that can be made by failure to use aids correctly; the damage that can be done by hasty training; the problems which crop up from lack of 'feel'.

Being aware of the aims, the first thing to do is to discover the horse's natural ability to walk. You may be able to assess this by lungeing the horse without the rider. This *can* be helpful, but so often the gait alters under the rider's weight, and may therefore have to be assessed again. The horse will show his true walk when he is at ease on a long rein, being encouraged to lower and stretch his head and neck. This helps relaxation of the back, allowing muscles the freedom to be used to the maximum. You can then see what scope the stride has, how far the hind legs come under the horse's body and whether the hind feet overtrack the imprints of the forefeet. This will then give you insight as to what you can expect of the horse, and how much you may demand from the rider in achieving what you want. So often, when the contact is taken up, freedom of stride is lost as the rider uses too much restraint or the horse draws back, losing forward inclination. Teaching the horse to accept the use of leg and hand together is dealt

46

with under Submission (see page 89). When this is achieved, the rider can expect acceptance of the bit combined with going forward, which will enable the horse to use the stride of which he is capable.

When working on the walk, the following inter-related factors should be assessed and monitored:

Speed. If the correct rhythm is to be maintained, the speed of the steps must be regulated. A hurried walk will often go out of rhythm, as can one which is insufficiently engaged.

Regularity. Regularity of the steps is essential to their quality. This ingredient can only be acquired from the horse being straight – accepting even contact of leg and hand – the hind feet always following in the tracks of the forefeet. Good balance is also necessary; the horse should carry equal weight over his four legs. Lack of engagement, being allowed to tip onto the forehand, leaning on the rider's hands, or not being supple enough can cause irregularities.

Rhythm. Rhythm goes hand in glove with regularity as, unless it is steady, regularity is lost. Establishing in the horse's mind the right speed, balance, straightness, regularity and rhythm takes months rather than weeks and the process can often be mislaid during the start of new exercises such as lateral work, collection and extension. Collection in particular, where steps are necessarily shortened and heightened, can invoke loss of sequence or regularity through tension or resistance. Many riders, allowing a dropping off of impulsion, fail to retain engagement, and there is a slowing of tempo (speed of steps, not forward speed) with a resultant walk that 'creeps' forward without activity. This sort of walk should be brought forward from better use of the leg aids, combined with submission to the bit.

Breaks. Breaks in walk occur frequently in a tense horse, causing anxiety all round. You will need to work through this with your pupils, helping them to obtain calmness through using their aids firmly, not taking them away, as many imagine.

Some will try to perform a type of Spanish walk.

If you are constantly training different horses, you will have many walks to deal with. An example would be the horse with a very 'big' walk who, when asked to shorten, either goes out of rhythm or tries to perform a type of 'Spanish walk'. This is when the forefeet are picked up high and dropped to the ground in a particularly slow rhythm, sometimes called 'goose stepping'. This can be quite difficult to correct, but keeping the horse in a rounder outline, making sure he is going forwards accepting leg and hand, does prevent it from forming into a habit.

Some horses will have great difficulty in overtracking. If this results from their conformation, it may always be a problem. However, many horses fail to overtrack because they are not being made to go forwards or they are hollowing their backs. Such hollowness will cause the head to be carried too high, and will probably also affect the stride.

At a later stage, when the horse is learning collection, the muscles in his back become contracted so, when the rider requires extension, there can be difficulty in persuading the horse to stretch. If you have built up to collection in the right way, varying the walk and not keeping the horse collected for too long, he should find the variation quite easy.

THE WALK

The Rider

The first, most important thing is to find out your horse's natural walk — the way he finds it easy. From this, you will determine what you can expect of him and what you may need to improve. Seeing the walk is obviously helpful, either on the lunge or, better still, loose in the field or school. By observing you can see whether he overtracks, and by how much; whether he moves straight; if the gait has natural balance and whether there are any obvious defects such as irregularities, uneven use of joints, dragging of feet, etc.

From watching, you should gain a fair idea of what to do when you ride so that you match what you have seen to the 'feel' the horse gives. It is very easy to spoil a walk and very difficult to improve a poor one. If your horse has a good walk then great care should be taken to preserve it, and not to cause faults by: overriding (driving the horse along unnecessarily with a lot of seat and leg); restricting the natural length of stride; allowing the horse to become unbalanced with too much weight on the forehand; forcing collection before there is adequate preparation or trying to keep the horse collected for too long at a time. It is all too easy to make mistakes but you have two ways to prevent them. You can be corrected by a trainer or you can discover how to perceive imperfections yourself. The latter option is the more satisfactory although, even with good perception, everyone can benefit through help from the ground.

Having discovered the horse's natural capability, your first job is to learn to ride 'on the aids', without destroying that feeling. As with all riding, there will be much trial and error but, if you feel the horse setting up too much resistance – swinging his hindquarters or altering his steps – you may be asking too much too quickly. Breaks in walk can result from tension. If you are satisfied that your aids are correct, then do not be 'blackmailed' into releasing the horse, but make him learn to accept what you have asked.

The 'feel' of a medium walk is the natural stride of the horse on the aids, so it should be purposeful and swinging along without tension. The 'feel' of collection is of slightly shorter steps, which spring more, with the horse's back arching under your seat. His hindquarters should feel as if they are stepping under the saddle, so that the forehand lifts and is lighter. The neck should feel more arched, the poll more flexed and the mouth (jaw) should be yielding. Extended walk gives the feeling of really 'going somewhere' – covering ground, with a reaching forward of the horse's neck and head, but there should be no dropping of weight onto the shoulders.

Free walk on a long rein should be very relaxed; the horse loosening his back muscles and simply striding forwards. He should reach out with his nose, lowering his neck as he does so, and should be allowed maximum length of rein (although light contact is maintained). Sometimes things will go wrong. Irregular steps are very common. If you feel any departure from the natural walk, the cause will very likely be some form of resistance to the aids. Evasions are many but any crookedness or stiffness can set off irregular steps, as can lack of proper engagement of the hindquarters, or any setting of the jaw against the hands.

When you come to collection, try to collect 'little and often' rather than attempting to make the horse go on for a long time. The latter approach will only cause him to feel 'trapped,' in which case he will almost certainly look for ways out. Some horses will react by turning 'nappy', others by 'shortening their necks' or trying to get 'above the bit', while some will learn to draw back into a 'creeping' walk in the wrong tempo. Collection should always feel forwards; the horse should never shuffle.

A horse with a good walk has a great asset, so try not to acquire one who has not. However, if you have one with the problem of under-tracking, then you should try to improve the walk through suppling exercises to make the horse step as far under himself as possible, and make sure there is good lengthening of the frame in extensions.

A relaxed free walk on a long rein.

THE TROT

The Judge

You should be thoroughly conversant with the following FEI definitions of the gait variants:

a) **Collected trot**. The horse, remaining 'on the bit' moves forward with his neck raised and arched. The hocks, being well engaged, maintain an energetic impulsion, thus enabling the shoulders to move with greater ease in any direction. The horse's steps are shorter than in the other trots, but he is lighter and more mobile.

b) **Working trot**. This is a pace between the collected and the medium trot, in which a horse, not yet trained and ready for collected movements, shows himself properly balanced and remaining 'on the bit', goes forward with even, elastic steps and good hock action. The expression 'good hock action' does not mean that collection is a required quality of working trot, it only underlines the importance of an impulsion originated from the activity of the hindquarters.

c) **Medium trot**. This is a pace between the working and the extended trot, but more 'round' than the latter. The horse goes forward with free and moderately extended steps and an obvious impulsion from the hindquarters. The rider allows the horse, re-maining 'on the bit', to carry his head a little more in front of the vertical than at the collected and the working trot, and allows him at the same time to lower his head and neck slightly. The steps should be as even as possible, and the whole movement balanced and unconstrained.

d) **Extended trot**. The horse covers as much ground as possible. Maintaining the same cadence, he lengthens his steps to the utmost as a result of great impulsion from the hindquarters. The rider allows the horse, remaining 'on the bit', without leaning on it, to lengthen his frame and gain ground. The forefeet should touch the ground on the spot towards where they are pointing. The movement of the fore- and hind legs should be similar (more or less parallel) in the forward movement of the extension. The whole movement should be well balanced and the transition to collected trot should be smoothly executed by taking more weight on the hindquarters.

From these definitions you should be able to assess whether the horse conforms satisfactorily to the requirements of the Level at which he is working (Preliminary, Novice, Elementary, Medium or Advanced). You will only know this from study and experience. It will help if you have trained a horse through the Levels yourself, as you will then know better what he can be expected to cope with.

As a judge, you should always be looking toward higher things, and thus giving encouragement through your marks to riders and horses who are aiming in the right direction – even if they fall short. Just because a horse is a novice it does not mean that he should be allowed to go on his forehand without correct engagement and balance. Any bearing down on the rider's hands or excessive weight being taken by the horse's shoulders should be penalised. Neither should you praise those who are 'trickling around the arena' – not asking for anything positive in case things go wrong.

Novice horses should be 'brought together' by the aids and, although they may be longer in the frame than a horse which has learned collection, a novice who can do so should not be penalised for showing a more advanced outline.

In the official BHS tests it is not a rule that riders should change their diagonals so, strictly speaking, they cannot be marked down for not doing so. However, as it is detrimental to the horse's training, a comment could be made in the rider's mark. In any case, it is only applicable in Preliminary and Novice tests, as from Elementary onwards the trot is ridden sitting.

Throughout the trot work, decisions will have to be made as to whether the relevant trot is being shown. Correct training may be determined by the ease with which the horse works. Resistances, irregularities, unlevelness and so on will come about from lack of balance, straightness, suppleness or acceptance of the aids. Therefore those faults will need to be penalised. This is especially important in the lower level tests, where the correct foundation should be laid. Riders in these tests may or may not be knowledgeable, but you will not be doing them a kindness by showing leniency to any fault which would prevent their progress up the scale. The trot work is vital, as it is a constituent of so many movements.

You will be hoping to see horses with big, scopey strides, good lift of shoulders and natural ability to flex the joints of the hind legs, all of whom are perfectly balanced in a rounded outline, unconstrained by their riders and keeping an exact rhythm from one movement to another. This picture of a good trot should be imprinted in your mind and, from this mental image, you will need to decide how far away from it each horse is. From this background image your brain, having 'computed' all possible faults, should almost automatically come up with a figure for each movement. This, of course, is not the end of the story as, in addition, comments should be made to explain the reason for the mark. This plainly requires a clear knowledge of cause and effect. For example, if a trot is unlevel, you will learn by experience whether the cause is almost certainly physical or the result of a one-sided-ness in the mouth – commonly known as 'bridle lameness' – which is a form of resistance. Or, to take an example of a different nature, whether a 'dwelling' trot results from the impulsion giving too much elevation to the steps rather than being directed into taking the horse forwards. Irregularities may be caused by poor ground, stiffness, resistance, or loss of balance, but loss or lack of rhythm generally arises because the desired speed has not been established or maintained.

TROT VARIANTS

Let us now consider the various trots.

Working Trot

In this, you would hope to see firstly, a horse who is going forwards with desire, having willingly obeyed the rider's leg aids. His energy should manifest itself in showing engagement of the hindquarters (active hind legs working under the horse – not 'out behind'). His steps should be even, elastic and active, and he should balanced at all times. He should have a rounded outline; his shoulders should have the freedom to allow the forelegs to lift and reach forwards; his neck should be slightly arched and the poll flexed, with his nose somewhat in front of the vertical. He should move around the arena within his capacity at the time. If his rider wishes to adjust the stride with half-halts to make movements easier, this should not be penalised unless it causes changes in rhythm or regularity.

Collected Trot

Because the horse is being 'gathered together' more than in working trot, the steps may be shorter and a little higher. Such steps can only come about if a greater degree of engagement takes place to lift the forehand, enabling the neck to show more arch and the poll to flex more, which brings the head to a vertical or almost vertical position. You will see a great deal of false collection – riders drawing their horses' necks up or back, or noses in, without sufficient engagement. You will also see a lot of restriction by riders' hands, causing short, shuffling steps and 'flat' steps with little elevation. Hollowness and resistance often result. These faults should be dealt with severely, as they are very detrimental to future work and can actually be distressing to the horse.

Medium Trot

This is a step on the road towards real extension, the horse being able, having been prepared by collection, to drive forward and lift at the same time into a bigger, more powerful stride. The frame of the horse should lengthen slightly, but the important points to note are whether the hindquarters can support the forehand in the bigger strides, and whether the horse can maintain his balance over the required distance.

Any hollowing or taking over of control by the horse are bad faults. Loss of engagement or balance sometimes makes horses 'wide behind', a rather unattractive fault and one which should never have a high mark, however flamboyant the fore-legs may look. (Although some horses are conformationally 'wide behind', their movement can be greatly improved through correct training.) With the bigger stride of the medium and extended gaits it is important to observe the use of the hind legs and not to be carried away with the forelegs, which may appear to be showing good steps. A comment used often is 'more in front than behind'. This is actually impossible; the forelegs cannot take a bigger steps than the hind legs, but they can come higher off the ground, which looks superficially im-pressive, but does not help the correct sequence of footfall.

Extensions

If the hind legs are properly active and the hindquarters engaged sufficiently to 'carry' the forehand, the horse will be in a position to give ultimate extension. He must also accept contained impulsion as he must allow his rider to 'store' it and then release only the amount he wants, when he wants.

Your job will be to ascertain whether the horse gives the maximum of which he is capable, to assess the quality of movement and to ascertain whether these requirements are sustained. It may also be necessary to assess whether a horse of limited extension is producing his maximum effort. Even if he does so this may not qualify him for a particularly high mark as it is probably short of the 'ultimate' picture, but he should not be automatically given a bad mark either.

Transitions and accuracy

The ability of the rider to start and finish a movement at an appointed place will depend upon the ability of the horse to re-balance himself from one size of stride pattern to another. This can only be achieved through good preparation from the rider and by the effective use of the half-halt. In the lower level tests you are able to accept progressive transitions as these enable the horse to learn to flow smoothly from one movement to another. Later on, transitions have to be more direct, which involves a higher degree of obedience and acceptance of aids. Where one transition is to be followed by another such as canter-walk-canter, the number of walk steps is of lesser im-portance than the quality of the transitions.

THE TROT

The Trainer

You should first of all be familiar with the FEI definitions (see page 52) and second, be able to see a correct trot sequence (one diagonal pair of legs coming to the ground simultaneously, and then the other). You will have many horses with very different strides to contend with in your career. There will be the ones you hope to see, with big, scopey strides showing plenty of freedom and lift, and there will be those who have strides inhibited by conformation defects or training errors.

Conformation defects can cause much trouble, for example horses with upright shoulders may be unable to lift and reach forward adequately with their forelimbs. Also, it can be exceedingly frustrating trying to achieve a good outline with a horse who is thick beneath the neck or sway-backed. Excessively long backs make engagement and lowering of hindquarters a difficulty.

Horses with natural rhythm have such an advantage over those without, as the trot gait depends so much on the exactness of its rhythm and regularity. One of your jobs will be to establish and enhance these two ingredients to such a degree that they evolve into springing steps of precision and distinction. This measured tread of flowing quality is called cadence.

A balanced trot cannot be developed without first setting a suitable speed. The only way of determining the speed for each individual horse will be to watch the action of the hind legs to see how far they come naturally under the horse's body

57

and how much natural joint flexion they show. The speed should be set to enable each horse to produce a stride which allows him to do this to his best ability. A horse with a scopey stride will be able to take quite a lot of impulsion without losing this ability. The less good the stride, the less impulsion the horse will be able to take to start with. In such cases, temporarily reducing the amount of actual forward momentum, whilst not allowing the horse to become inactive, will encourage a greater degree of joint flexion to be developed. Some horses may have to work at a seemingly very slow speed early in their careers in order to build up the capacity of the hind legs to lift the horse and take him forward in a balanced manner. Once this is achieved, the lift produced by flexion of the joints makes the gait more active and assists balance. Therefore, when more impulsion is put to the gait, the horse will be better able to cover ground, show freedom and perform gait variants.

If the correct speed and balance have been established, the horse should find it relatively easy to maintain a regular stride and a precise rhythm. It will be most important to observe any deficiences in the stride. Each hind leg must follow in the track of the appropriate foreleg; each step must equal its partner; each hind leg must flex equally; each diagonal pair of legs must come to the ground together, with a moment of suspension between them. The horse's back should be free from constraint so that it is able to swing easily, allowing maximum use of the hindquarters. The tail moving from side to side in rhythm with the stride is evidence that this is occurring. The horse's shoulders should lift so that he can reach out with his forelegs, but their movement should not be exaggerated; they should work harmoniously with his hind legs in a kind of 'cycling' action.

You will, of course, be aware of the need to change diagonals in rising trot to develop the horse's back muscles evenly. Many riders do have a problem in knowing which diagonal they are on. Everyone has their own method of teaching recognition. Some will teach the rider to look down to see which foreleg is doing what until they can associate it with the sensation of the movement. Others, of whom I am one, dislike the looking down method. I prefer to make riders look up and concentrate on the feel right from the start. I then make them tell me which leg is doing what by calling out 'left, right, left,' etc., until the feeling is ingrained.

COMMON FAULTS IN TROT

'Dwelling'

A fault which can occur as a result of the endeavour to evoke suspension between the diagonal steps is, in fact, over-suspension. A natural moment of suspension will carry the horse forwards. In a 'dwelling' trot that moment is prolonged without the inclination to go forwards. The rider may create this by driving the impulsion into hands which overdo the half-halt, or do not allow the energy to go forwards. Some horses will use such a trot as an evasion to going forwards in a way which involves more effort than they are prepared to give. It can be difficult to get such horses out of the habit and they will probably require a lot of driving forwards, even out of their natural rhythm, in order to override the upward inclination.

Improving horses with poor trots with little or no natural suspension between the steps is a challenge and possibly not worth the effort if aiming for advanced dressage. Only by establishing a very exact rhythm in good balance will you have any chance of acquiring what you want and, even then, there is a very fine line regarding the appropriate amount of energy. Too much can send the trot 'flat', too little, and it will not spring at all.

Uneven and Unlevel Gait

You will come across uneven and unlevel trots and you must be able to determine the cause. Uneven steps may result from resistance in the mouth or stiffness. Unlevelness can mean that the horse is lame or has some physical problem, but it can also be that he is very 'one-sided', his muscles having developed unevenly. Horses are quite often what is known as 'bridle-lame', meaning that the acceptance of the bit is unequal, causing impulsion travelling forwards to be accepted on one side of the mouth and 'blocked' on the other. You must learn to see whether this is happening and then know how, by using flexions, to loosen the 'set' area (the poll and lower jaw) and thus release the blocked energy. Some horses will show persistent unlevelness behind until they are properly suppled when, if the cause was in fact some stiffness, it will disappear. Experience will teach you to differentiate between those horses who are actually lame and those who are merely unlevel.

OUTLINE

Whether the horse is at a novice or advanced stage one thing should be the same – he should never be allowed to take more weight on his shoulders than over the rest of his body. Novice horses will necessarily be in a longer outline than advanced horses but, from day one, you should encourage your pupils to engage the hindquarters. The whole future of the trot depends on it and, without engagement, the horse's back cannot become rounded, the forehand cannot lift or lighten, nor can the horse carry himself. Resistances are so often caused by lack or loss of balance, which can be a direct result of losing engagement.

The development of the trot by greater impulsion and collection as time goes on produces greater quality, but only if engagement has been properly obtained and maintained. A rounded outline with good submission gradually takes the rider towards the higher degrees of collection (piaffe and passage, together with the connecting transitions). Only from correct engagement, collection and contained energy can the horse ultimately give the sort of extensions required. You will be responsible for this development; knowing when to progress to the next stage.

GAIT VARIATION

Part of the development of trot will involve variations within the gait; shortening and lengthening, which teaches the horse the first steps towards collection and extension. He should perform these variations with progressive transitions from and to a working gait. This work should be limited to a degree commensurate with the level of balance at the time. These variations cannot be achieved successfully except through the use of the half-halt.

Collection

A collected trot should have the energy of the working gait, but with the horse more 'brought together'. His hindquarters should be more engaged to lift the forehand, his neck thus coming higher and more arched, with more flexion at the poll and the nose in a vertical or almost vertical position. The steps should have plenty of spring, with a clear moment of suspension, but they should also be covering ground and taking the horse forwards.

The steps should not alter during the lateral work, but should remain at the height of the preceding trot. On no account should the rider's hands be allowed to restrict, draw back or cause a 'flattening' of the steps. Pupils should be encouraged to work without stirrups for a short time during a lesson. This will produce better depth in the saddle and more security. Any bumping about, loss of balance or collapsing of the position will inevitably be reflected in the horse's way of going.

Extensions

Suppleness and security in the saddle are particularly relevant in extended trot, where there is an enormous amount of movement that needs absorbing. It is very easy to unbalance the horse and cause breaks of rhythm by looseness of the seat. Stirrups are often lost or the reins used for support which of course hinders both horse and rider. The rider should be encouraged to develop the strength for this exercise by riding without stirrups but only for a short period. Any muscle strain may recur and recovery from it can be a lengthy business.

Once collection is becoming established, work can begin on medium and extended gaits. A degree of collection will have put the horse in a stage of balance where, if he is asked to reach for a bigger stride, he should be able to do so. When the horse has fully grasped the medium trot, he can be gradually brought to the first stage of extension – the ultimate stage being reserved for the final part of his training. This will be when he has reached maximum, resistant-free, controlled impulsion.

In all extended work the horse should show a lengthening of his frame. This should not come about by giving away the rein but by allowing the impulsion greater expression. The horse should never fall onto his forehand nor lose engagement. Particular attention should be given to the manner in which the transitions are ridden before and after the extension.

THE TROT

The Rider

You should first make yourself familiar with the FEI definitions of the trots variants used in tests (see page 52). Secondly, you will need to assess what sort of trot your horse has. It always helps to see a horse loose to observe his natural gait, and this gives a picture of his ability to add to the feeling he gives when ridden. If you have a young horse who appears to have a lovely trot loose, but he seems to lose it when you ride do not be dismayed. This should be only temporary. As he learns to cope with your weight and aids, the good movement should return. As with all the gaits, your job is to preserve and improve upon the horse's natural ability. You should begin by putting the horse in a balance in which he can hold a regular, rhythmic stride. Setting a speed at which your horse can learn to carry himself and you without difficulty will be your primary concern.

THE AIDS

The horse will have to learn to accept control from the use of your outside rein assisted by the inside rein, which also asks for a flexion to the way you are going. He must also accept your inside leg, which will be ensuring that he goes forwards and gives a bend. At no time should he lean on the inside rein or leg. There are two very useful exercises which will teach him not to do this — Give and Re-take the Rein (see page 150) and Leg-yielding (see page 198). Your inside leg will need help from the outside one to keep the horse going forward, asking for and maintaining a bend, and controlling the hindquarters in general.

The Seat

Your seat will have a great influence over the trot, so development of depth and security is very important. Trot is not always the easiest gait to sit, and any untoward bumping about or loss of balance can be very upsetting for the horse and possibly destroy the gait. Therefore, in the early stages, it may be wise to use rising trot to allow the horse's back muscles to develop without hindrance.

In trot, as you will discover, the horse uses himself with alternate diagonal pairs of legs: off fore and near hind, near fore and off hind. Each pair touch the ground simultaneously and, as they do, you will, if using rising trot, either rise or sit. If you are rising to the trot, be certain to change your diagonal as you change the rein. This is done by sitting for an extra step before rising again. Failure to do this encourages unequal development of the back muscles, which leads eventually to stiffness and one-sidedness.

When learning to sit to the trot, it is useful to ride an older horse, whose back will be less affected. Being lunged without reins or stirrups by someone knowledgeable can be extremely beneficial.

Contact

It is not always easy to understand how to get a horse between leg and hand. In trot, this often seems very hard as there is so much movement which can dislodge your position. It is most important, however, to be able to maintain contact with your legs around the horse while your hands take up and retain a contact with his mouth. Keeping this contact is essential to successful training.

QUALITIES OF THE TROT

Regularity

If you have set the speed at which you want the horse to work, and have found a compatible rhythm, your attention should next focus on developing an exactness of stride which will enable you to perform all movements and variations in the gait. This exactness will depend upon your control, your ability to anticipate loss of balance and therefore prevent it, plus immediate recognition of any alteration in the stride caused by stiffness or resistance.

Rhythm and cadence

Regularity and rhythm go hand in glove; but cadence may follow only when they are combined with impulsion, suppleness and good acceptance of the aids. The horse should appear to move effortlessly, never altering the steadiness of his stride. If you are lucky, you may find a horse with an inbuilt rhythm, which you must strive to retain. If you are less fortunate, then the making of the trot will be dependent on your ability to feel what is necessary to produce clear diagonal steps with a moment of suspension between them.

GAIT VARIATIONS

When you come to teaching the horse shortening and lengthening in preparation for collection and extension, your powers of 'feel', together with well co-ordinated aids, will be very necessary. You should aim first for the preliminary 'collecting' of the horse, which will involve astute use of the half-halt. This will help him to engage his hindquarters, making it easier for him to propel himself forwards in a balanced way. Do beware of overuse of the hands, since this will only prevent freedom and may cause short steps lacking in energy, and resistances.

You may find that, by temporarily reducing energy within the horse, although *not* to the extent of accepting inactivity, he will find it easier to learn to adjust his stride for collection. This is not a problem. If it makes things easier for him, it is often better to teach the horse what you want less impulsively and then build up the impulsion again later on. With shortening and lengthening you should only ask for a few strides at a time to begin with, and then return to the basic gait. Once the horse has learned to shorten his steps, he should quite soon be able to lengthen also, as he will have learned through the half-halt to engage more and accept a higher degree of the combined use of leg and hand. As you ask him to take a bigger stride, he will be in a balance from which he can comply, and you will be able to contain the impulsion and bring him back to the original gait.

OUTLINE

In all your work you will, of course, expect less from the novice horse than you will from the advanced. At the novice stage, however, you should still expect the horse to go with hind-quarters well engaged, in a rounded outline, with his neck rising from the withers into an arch along the crest, his head being flexed at the poll with his nose in front of the vertical. At no time should there be weight bearing down on the shoulders or any leaning on the hands for support. This basic shape should be kept throughout the horse's training, the only differences being that, as weight is transferred further onto the hindquarters as the result of collection, the forehand will lighten even more. A greater arch of the neck will gradually result, accompanied by even more flexion at the poll, with the horse's head becoming vertical or almost vertical to the ground. The horse's back should feel vibrant beneath your seat and, if the horse is working correctly, he will be easy to sit into.

RESISTANCES

Unless you are a most careful and talented rider there will be many resistances to deal with as, while the horse is learning, he will become unbalanced, confused or even dislike what he is being asked to do. Learning to cope with evasions is every rider's problem. When work is difficult it is understandable that the horse will sometimes object. It is easy to get down-hearted and become negative with the aids, especially if the horse is persistant in his resistance. It is important to be firm so long as you are certain that you have made your wishes clear. If you are in doubt always go back a stage to something easier for a while. Never enter into an argument unless you are sure you can win but then be determined that you will. Your horse will rely on you. You will have to help him through by patience, repetition and reward. The security of your position and the effective influence of your aids will be the route to producing trot work of high quality, which will carry you in due course from Novice Level to Advanced.

THE CANTER

The Judge

You should be thoroughly conversant with the following FEI definitions of the gait variants:

a) **Collected canter**. The horse, remaining 'on the bit' moves forward with his neck raised and arched. The collected canter is marked by the lightness of the forehand and the engagement of the hindquarters: ie. is characterised by supple, free and mobile shoulders and very active quarters. The horse's strides are shorter than at the other canters, but he is lighter and more mobile.

b) **Working canter**. This is a pace between the collected and the medium canter, in which a horse not yet trained and ready for collected movements, shows himself properly balanced and, remaining 'on the bit', goes forward with even light cadenced strides and good hock action. The expression 'good hock action' does not mean that collection is a required quality of working canter. It only underlines the importance of an impulsion originated from the activity of the hindquarters.

c) **Medium canter**. This is a pace between the working and the extended canter. The horse goes forward with free, balanced and moderately extended strides and an obvious impulsion from the hindquarters. The rider allows the horse, remaining 'on the bit' to carry his head a little more in front of the vertical than at the collected and working canter, and allows him at the same time to lower his head and neck slightly. The strides should be long and as even as possible, and the whole movement balanced and unconstrained.

66

Collected canter – Jane Bredin on Goya

d) **Extended canter**. The horse covers as much ground as possible. Maintaining the same rhythm, he lengthens his strides to the utmost, without losing any of his calmness and lightness, as a result of great impulsion from the hindquarters. The rider allows the horse, remaining 'on the bit' without leaning on it, to lower and extend his head and neck, the tip of his nose pointing more or less forward.

Bearing in mind the above definitions, you will be involved in assessing three main points and ensuring that:

1) The canter remains in the correct rhythm, that is, three-beat.

2) The rider is asking the horse to perform the canter required; collected, medium, etc.

3) The horse remains in this canter throughout the designated movement, and is straight.

The first point is the most vital, as it is the purity of the gait which is its basis, so any failure in this department not only affects future work, but will cause the movement to lose marks. You will see the rhythm being lost as the result of poor balance, crookedness, stiffness or hollowing, inadequate engagement or impulsion, or restriction by the rider. Horses with little or no suspension between the strides are more prone to a four-beat canter, but you must train your eye very carefully to ensure that you do not make a mistake on this point. Watching for the hind and foreleg which should come to the ground together may make this clear.

Assessment of which canter the horse is in may sound ob-vious, as it is laid down in the test but, unfortunately, riders do not always achieve what the test demands. You must there-fore decide whether the particular canter variant is adequate for what it should be as well as for the stage of training (thus the degree of medium canter for an Elementary horse will be less than for a Medium horse, etc.). There may be a certain difficulty in differentiating between medium and extended work, as some horses are unable to produce any real difference. You will need to observe closely to determine whether this difference has been shown. Part of the difference should be the alteration or lengthening of the frame, which should be pro-

Canter – Carl Hester on Otto

gressively greater to match the size of the stride. The difference of stride between the working and collected gaits is not so great as between working and medium, where a distinctly larger stride is desired. Working canter should show good forward activity in a balanced, rounded outline, which should be seen throughout the work. Unfortunately, in the process of endeavouring to obtain collection, the forward inclination is often lost through too strong a use of the rider's hands without sufficient support from the legs. This may result in a 'drawing back' or 'shortening' of the horse's neck. The steps become restricted, dropping in height and the gait may then very likely become four-beat. In the medium and extended work there is often failure by the rider to maintain enough engagement hence, instead of the hindquarters lifting the stride and taking the horse forward, balance is lost and weight falls onto the forehand. You must be able to notice how this inhibits the stride, preventing any real quality from being shown. Good transitions before and after any variation in the gait are essential.

Maintaining the required canter throughout the movement is achievable if the horse is able, through training, to sustain it, and is straight enough. Many problems in canter stem from crookedness. You will often have to make remarks about the quarters being in. If this is so, they will be unable to engage properly, which clearly affects the whole canter work. Also, in this case, weight is generally taken by the horse's outside shoulder, which leads to many other problems. The sort of thing that occurs is that, in order to keep the horse to a line, the rider uses the inside rein too much causing more bend in the horse's neck than in the rest of his body. Also, because the weight is uneven, balance is gradually lost. This can cause breaks in the gait or difficulties with the steering. Any lack of straightness or balance opens the door for difficulty to creep in, and anything which the horse finds awkward can cause resistances or breaks in the gait. The correction for the rider to make is to take shoulder-in position which, if the aids are used correctly, brings the shoulders into a position in front of the hindquarters. This is a temporary correction. Some riders use quite a lot of 'position'. I have known this to be faulted by judges and, in some cases, if you consider it excessive this is right. However, if the 'positioning' is quite small this should be perfectly acceptable. This is perhaps one example of why judges should ride as well as judge, so that they are better placed to assess the necessity or otherwise of such measures.

Throughout the canter work you will want to see the horse 'bound', with clear, expressive strides and a good moment of suspension. Without this moment the horse will be unable to cover ground in the lateral work or to accomplish the flying changes correctly. He should work with lowered hindquarters, never being 'croup high', as this seriously hinders the work and, especially, makes canter pirouettes difficult.

THE CANTER

The Trainer

For definitions of canter variants, see page 66. You will expect your pupils and the judges to understand the correct sequence of footfall for canter and you will want both to recognise at once when this is lost. It will be your job to teach pupils what is a good canter and help them with all the ensuing problems.

Assuming that you yourself know the *feeling* of when a horse is sufficiently balanced to show a clear rhythm of stride, with a moment of suspension, then you will assist the pupil by your ability also to *see* this. Most canters start on the forehand and tend to consist of long, even raking, strides. It requires a rider with stable seat and effective aids to assist the horse to adjust his balance and learn to engage his hindquarters. If your pupil is weak in this department, you may wish initially to strengthen and deepen his seat by working him on the lunge on a schoolmaster. There is nothing more difficult than trying to get a horse off his forehand with a weak rider. As you teach your pupils how to sit in canter so that they do not hinder progress, you may also have to arrive at a steadier speed by short periods of canter with transitions to trot between, merely to give the horse a chance to re-balance himself. This allows time to correct co-ordination of the pupil's aids, and any resistances by the horse. Although you will have worked on half-halts in trot, the greater speed of canter presents its own problems. If the rider is able, half-halts should be employed to make improvements. If your pupil is more novice, he will

71

need help to discover how to use them. Untutored, a novice may merely pull on the reins, making the horse throw his head up and go hollow. As any hollowing may cause strain to the horse's back this must be avoided, and emphasis placed on keeping the horse in a correct outline.

You will be aware of the necessity of making the horse go forwards in order to maintain correct sequence of footfall. Also, you must help your pupils to feel for, and maintain, a regular rhythm. Naturally, everyone should know how to ask the horse to canter on a specified leg but, so often, pupils are not clear with their aids, nor do they know which leg they are on. Young horses and novice riders may be allowed to canter initially with an outward bend to help both to achieve the correct lead. Once this is done, the correct aids and bend must be introduced. Only in the case of a particularly stubborn or ill-trained animal who has always been allowed to canter on his favoured leg (an action which will have compounded any inherent 'one-sidedness') can you allow an outward bend to be retained for any length of time. Use of the schooling whip on the horse's outside shoulder may help to eradicate this problem.

Getting the horse straight is one of the chief problems in canter. You may be aware that the use of shoulder-in 'position' is a highly effective means of dealing with crookedness. One of your tasks will be to teach pupils to feel where the horse is 'escaping'. He may put more weight on one shoulder than the other, or his hindquarters may fall in or swing out. If a true bend − that is to say, a uniform curve throughout the length of the horse − is achieved and kept, then it is relatively simple to take a shoulder-in position. Often the bend is incorrect so, when the rider tries to take 'position', there is a loophole through which the horse can escape. One recurrent fault I find is that the rider's inside leg is not used properly on the girth but either draws back or swings and there is therefore no stability for the bend.

Only good, co-ordinated aids will enable the pupil to obtain 'positioning' but, once it is understood and accomplished, correction can be made at any time during canter; coming into halt, from rein-back and so on. Of course, being able to keep the canter straight is vital to all the work from simple, straight-forward circles to pirouettes and flying changes.

When the time comes to help pupils ride canter movements in tests, do remember to position yourself at C, where the judge will be. This applies at some time to all the work because it is only from there that you will really be able to see the straightness properly, and also whether the gait variants have been clearly defined. From that vantage point nothing much can be missed but, in any case, you do need to see movements ridden as the judge will see them.

It requires a rider with a stable seat and effective aids to assist the horse to adjust his balance.

THE CANTER

The Rider

First of all you will need to understand the correct sequence of footfalls and know exactly what is required in tests (see the FEI definitions, page 66). Having read the definitions you must ensure that you are clear in your mind what the four canter variants are; what they look like ridden by others, and what they feel like. It can be remarkably instructive simply to watch your horse in the field, cantering about in his natural state.

BALANCE

You may have noticed whether your horse is normally well balanced or whether he is inclined to put weight onto his shoulder. The former is clearly better than the latter, but at least you will know what to expect. Developing his balance with you in the saddle will be your prime concern initially, then teaching him which leg to canter on and associating it with your aids. It is very important that he learns to strike off equally well to both directions and does so without having to 'fall' into canter from an increased speed or by leaning to the side. A young horse starting off may do both of these things and may also be bent away from the leading leg but, as soon as possible, the correct bend and aids should be used. Many riders use more outside leg than inside to get canter. This has two undesirable results – one being that it encourages the horse to lean in and the other that it can make the hindquarters come

74

in. This means that the hind legs are not following the forelegs;
the first cause of crookedness in canter.

THE AIDS

The inside leg should be chiefly responsible for sending the
horse forward so, provided the outside leg (used lightly) tells
the horse which leg to canter on, the inside one simply says
'do it'. Any other alteration in pressure or placement of the
inside leg (which should be on the girth) in canter can confuse
the horse, causing him to swing his quarters, change leg,
become disunited and so on. The outside rein controls the gait
while the inside rein directs and asks for flexion.

It may seem too obvious to state that you must know which
leg your horse is on in canter, but it is surprising how many
riders are not sure. Looking down is unbalancing. Allowing
your horse to go even a short distance on a lead you have not
asked for is bad training. If you wish to ride tests you will
want your horse to be ultra-obedient, so it is essential that you
train yourself to recognise at once what is going on underneath
you.

PROBLEMS IN CANTER

Canter is a complex gait, and you may come across various
problems.

Crookedness
This is a very common problem. You will recognise it if you
are sensitive to the weight that the horse may try to put on one
shoulder or the other and to the position of the hindquarters.
Be careful to notice whether you really do have a uniform bend
through the horse. Bending the horse's neck too much is one of
the main causes of crookedness.

Loss of engagement
Losing engagement is also the root cause of many difficulties.
You should know when this is lost by the lack of 'bounce' or
'spring' which the canter should give if it is correct. Any
feeling of being 'too close to the ground', with little or no
suspension, will almost surely mean that the hindquarters are

not doing their job. More effective use of the leg aids to get the horse going forward more actively should get you back on the right track.

(Losing suspension can also be caused by collecting too much from the hands without enough drive from seat and legs. This makes the strides shorten, but at the expense of losing energy and, therefore, height.)

Hollowing

If you feel the horse hollowing his back away from you, or fighting to get his head 'above the bit', it may be wise to start whatever you were trying to do again, making sure that you first 'round' the horse and get him to accept the aids. Any movement in a hollow outline will be poor and can put potentially injurious strain on the horse's back muscles and loins: it should therefore be avoided.

WORKING CANTER

The feel of a good working canter should always be three-beat, with a distinct moment of suspension between each stride. Until the horse is balanced underneath you and you have some semblance of control, this feeling may be obscure. It is important that you arrive at a speed at which the horse can sustain a canter in self-carriage as soon as possible so that a rhythm can be established. Thereafter, all variations of canter and all movements should be in the same rhythm.

Once your horse has attained the degree of balance whereby he can sustain an active canter and negotiate the school performing straight, smooth transitions, he should be ready to begin learning to respond to the collecting aids.

CANTER VARIANTS

Collection

'Bringing the horse together' will often produce problems of resistance. If the horse has already learned some collection in walk and trot and will accept a degree of half-halt, these resistances can be overcome without too much difficulty. To be able to collect, the horse must have a degree of suppleness, so that he can give the lateral bend needed towards the leading leg, and can be asked to round his back through engagement of the hindquarters. As more engagement is asked for, so better acceptance of the bit will have to follow if the quality of the canter is to be retained. You will need to feel for any serious resistance in the mouth which might block impulsion, and be able to loosen a crossing or set jaw by quiet alternate action of the hands. This will move the bit, making the horse chew and, in turn, the poll will also have to give, providing the loosening needed. The horse's neck, also, can be a seat of resistance and set muscles can be loosened by alternate flexions. Suppling exercises in general (especially shoulder-in at trot) will help your canter work.

Until such collection is accomplished it would be unwise to attempt lengthening, as this would invite loss of balance. Only when the horse can sustain engagement in self-carriage should he be asked to produce a medium or extended stride.

Medium Canter

The medium canter strides will derive from basic balance, straightness and acceptance of the aids so that, by merely asking for a bigger stride, the horse will be able to comply. You must make sure that you adhere to the rhythm you have set and that this is not lost in the transitions. When the horse responds to your leg aids, your arms and hands must allow a little lengthening of the frame – but beware of allowing any weight to fall onto the forehand. If your work is correct, you should feel a longer moment of suspension.

Extension

The extended canter is a larger version of the medium stride and should cover considerable ground during the period of suspension. While you must make sure that you allow more lengthening of the frame, do not let the horse get away from you or try to gallop off, as this would take you away from the correct sequence of footfalls for canter.

Riding the canter variants

Showing the difference between the four canter variants re-quired in tests can only be achieved from first having a correct canter and then being able to start and finish a movement with a clear, resistance-free transition. These canter variants will be progressive in the early stages, that is to say, the size of stride will gradually increase or reduce. Later on, you may expect to obtain extended canter almost immediately from collection and to return in one or two strides (see Half-halts, page 169). This will enable you to show greater accuracy and to start and finish at a marker. In all transitions it is important to be very conscious of the use of your seat and legs to keep the hindquarters under the horse and prevent any weight tipping onto the forehand. Far too often one sees a rider trying to bring the horse back from an extended canter more by the reins than the leg, thereby causing all manner of problems. Also, if you allow yourself to be tipped forwards in canter you immediately lose strength of position.

In this medium canter the horse does not show quite enough lengthening of his frame.

PART FOUR
The Effects of the Aids

It's always good to win!

INFLUENCE OF THE AIDS

The Judge

In tests, influence of the aids comes under obedience. In the light of this, your assessments may possibly be influenced by the result more than the cause, as this will be the more obvious. Also, whether or not the horse accepts the aids is so dependent on how they are given. The causes of resistance are therefore predominantly the fault of the rider. Even so, you have to mark what you see from the horse – but take this into account in your end mark for the rider.

Since resistance to aids is almost entirely the result of poor or faulty training, it should be looked upon as unsatisfactory. There can be no progression towards Grand Prix unless the horse willingly submits to his rider's aids, so marks should be given accordingly. No-one wants to give poor marks but too much leniency in this area of the work may mislead the competitor and can be a disservice to him. It may well be better in the long run to make competitors take a good look at themselves and their problems at an early stage than to allow incorrect development which is far harder to correct later.

One other point to bear in mind is that some competitors actually ask very little of their horses, but rather 'con' the horse round the arena. Use your experience to determine this, so that you do not get carried away and give high marks. There is quite a difference between this 'trickling about' not really quite 'on the aids' and having the horse really between leg and hand.

INFLUENCE OF THE AIDS

The Trainer

You may find it helpful to ride each horse to discover his reaction to aids applied. Many horses are far less responsive to the leg than they first appear, and many are very 'dead' in the mouth. Only by getting a reaction first from the leg, followed by a yielding to contact taken on the mouth will you be setting off on the right road. As a trainer you should have acquired the knack of overcoming any resistances put up by the horse, but teaching this to others is often a lengthy and perhaps frustrating business. The whole secret lies in the ability of a pupil to co-ordinate the aids. Some can naturally apply them effectively and others, however hard they try, cannot. Your aim will be to help them as much as you can, first in understanding the necessity and secondly in the accomplishment. So far as the horse is concerned, he will only accept what to him is acceptable -- and this means teaching pupils how to be tactful, sympathetic and yet firm.

Naturally, this takes time and patience. There must be a clear understanding on the part of the riders of the precise aids to be used for whatever they are trying to do, and these aids must be used consistently. It will be a major part of your job to make sure this happens.

For the rider, especially the novice, the means of communication bring about endless problems. To start with, limbs seem to defy the brain, not doing what they are told, and accumulating sufficient knowledge is, in itself, a trial. After all, the aids are only the result of the brain telling the body to give them, so the right messages have to be transmitted. You can support your clear explanations of what to expect and what to do with visual demonstrations; by riding yourself, making one pupil watch another, or by the use of film. When the basics have been thoroughly comprehended by both rider and horse,

Visual demonstrations are a great help.

the future may well be dependent upon the sensitivity and 'feel' of the rider; the ability to use the aids in such a way that they have the correct influence, thus making it possible for the horse to respond in the right way. One point to bear in mind is that of teaching good preparation, so that the horse is placed in the best position to answer what he is being asked.

You, yourself, will need to know how to get over the problems of the various evasions. Horses will not necessarily accept readily what is asked, particularly when the more demanding stages are reached. It will be your task to check continually that the basics are correct, that the horse is allowing himself to be ridden firmly from the leg to the hand and that he does not get away with anything. Also, that your training makes allowances for the necessary build up of the horse's physical strength and mental understanding, so that there can be no reason why he will not be submissive to the rider's wishes. Riders, similarly, need a level of development before the right kind of rapport can be expected between the two.

INFLUENCE OF THE AIDS
The Rider

What, I wonder, do you understand by the influence of the aids? I think this may depend upon your expectations. For instance, if you merely want to ride around the countryside enjoying the feel of a horse while admiring the view, there will be no need for the horse to be more than well mannered, answering a slight leg aid to go forwards or a feel on the mouth for slowing or turning. This is perfectly acceptable, provided that your horse is also enjoying himself! He may do so if he is able to answer without difficulty when you ask him to do something. This sounds reasonable, you say, and of course this is what you always do. For your horse's sake I hope it is. Sadly, however, many riders are oblivious to some of the horse's basic needs: that of balance, which will enable him to carry himself and you safely and easily; that of understanding, so that when you use your legs he will answer and go forwards. How often do you see other riders kicking incessantly at their horses' sides? Is this pleasant for the horse? Much better to give him a little basic training and teach him to answer the leg properly. Also, understanding the use of the bit must be very puzzling to the poor horse. He may get someone who rides with a loose rein: 'How nice for him', you say. But what happens when the rider has to take some contact because of the need to stop suddenly, to turn out of someone's way or to prevent the horse from falling into a hole? The bit suddenly jars against the horse's mouth or tongue, perhaps causing quite a lot of pain. How often does your horse throw up his head against the feel of the bit? What I am getting at is that, for even the least demanding sort of riding, the horse needs to be taught how you want him to reply to your needs.

If you are already a competition rider, you will have had to learn the aids for negotiating the arena and for different movements. There are really only a few basic aids, which are applied in various combinations with variations of pressure to produce the different movements and exercises. The basic aids are:

The influence of your seat and weight from a correct and well maintained position in the saddle.

The outside rein controls the speed, tempo, rhythm and assists the inside rein.

The inside leg used on the girth sends the horse forwards and holds the bend.

The inside rein asks for flexion (bend) and directs the horse, with assistance from the outside rein.

The outside leg controls the hindquarters, preventing them from going out, helps to bend the horse round the inside leg, and helps with the impulsion.

The voice is used for praise or as a reprimand (although you should be aware that use of the voice during a test is penalised).

Both legs are responsible for making the horse go forwards and maintaining impulsion and engagement. A horse does not understand what kicking means, so has to be taught from the combined use of voice, legs and whip, followed by praise when the result is correct.

The hands are responsible for controlling the impulsion requested by the legs, and must allow freedom of the gaits. The only means you have of physically controlling forward movement of the horse is through your hands, the reins and the bit (although the voice can help). The horse's reaction to the feel of the bit may be to ignore it or to fight it. When the horse fights the bit, he is resisting the hand aids. He needs therefore to be taught how to accept the feel of it when it is used. Now comes the difficult part! You will readily visualise that it will be no good if the horse only answers the leg aids but not the hand aids, or vice versa. There needs to be an acceptance of the two at the same time. This is only possible if you co-ordinate the use of your aids, asking the horse to go forward from your legs into a contact on his mouth, to which he must yield. So many riders fall into the trap of not obtaining a yielding before they lighten their contact. The lightening is the reward to the horse for this yielding and allows him forwards. Lightening the contact is not loosening or giving away the rein, nor should it allow the horse to fall on his forehand. Obtaining a yield without maintaining engagement and impulsion will only result in losing its effect, and may cause opposition from the horse in the form of him hollowing his outline. Hollowing usually occurs because the rein aids are used without adequate support from the legs. This makes the horse raise his head and come 'above the bit'. Once in this position it is easy for him to evade and rider control is, therefore, lost. Some riders seem to be under the misapprehension that a loose rein is more acceptable to the horse than a contact. Of course the right kind of contact is essential but the inevitable picking up of a loose rein is much more likely to cause pain than a more constant pressure. It is not always easy to feel when the horse is hollow or when he is sufficiently round and, therefore, whether to use aids more or less firmly. The feel of his back should provide a clue; if it feels as though it is sinking beneath your seat he is probably hollow whereas it feels firm yet supple when he is round.

Until these basics are understood by both parties, progress will be very limited. Only by gradual development of a combined use of the aids (see Half-halts, page 169) will you form a capacity to 'talk' effectively to your horse and expect him to be able to respond.

As you will know if you have ridden tests, a high degree of control is necessary, both for negotiating such a small space and riding accurately through the movements. This is only achievable if you have reached a high level of understanding, making it possible for your horse to respond easily and willingly to all the aids you give him.

OBEDIENCE AND SUBMISSION

The Judge

The FEI rules have the following to say about submission:

> 1) Submission does not mean a truckling subservience, but an obedience revealing its presence by a constant attention, willingness and confidence in the whole behaviour of the horse as well as by the harmony, lightness and ease he is displaying in the execution of the different movements. The degree of submission is also manifested by the way the horse accepts the bridle; with a light and soft contact and supple poll, or with resistance to or evasion of the rider's hands; being either 'above the bit' or 'behind the bit' respectively.
>
> 2) Putting out the tongue, keeping it above the bit or drawing it up altogether, as well as grinding the teeth and swishing the tail are mostly signs of nervousness, tenseness or resistance on the part of the horse and must be taken into account by the judges in their marks for the movement concerned as well as in the collective mark for 'submission'.

One of your chief tasks will be to evaluate the degree of obedience by the horse to the rider's aids. This acceptance or submission will be obvious within each movement ridden. Any resistances will lose marks, particularly if they are frequent. Resistance to leg aids manifests itself in reluctance to go forwards or to engage the hindquarters, and in many other ways detailed further on (see Evasions and Resistances, page 92). All resistance makes the picture unattractive and is detrimental to performance.

I think it is important to be able to measure degrees of resistance to training and the possible outcome for that horse's future. Any repetitive reluctance is clearly unsatisfactory, but a momentary one caused by a short loss of balance or perhaps a misunderstanding is plainly less destructive. Naturally, you should also relate your evaluation to the level of training. The expected degree of submission in a horse at Novice Level would be less than one of Advanced standard.

Resistances can occur for so many reasons. So often they are simply the result of lack of preparation. It is vital for you to know the position in which the horse should be prior to each movement so that he may have the best chance to perform it. If you believe that a rider has done the best they can, any failure may be due to lack of training. This may result in mental confusion by the horse or he may physically not be able to respond. It is up to you to decide. Active resistance such as evasions of the bit or tail swishing are easy to see but quite often the horse puts up a passive resistance where he simply puts as little as possible into his work. This kind of resistance will not earn high marks but sometimes comes out higher than expected because nothing very obvious went wrong.

You will also find that you will have to take into account the way the horse is ridden. If you feel that the rider's aids are not clear or are poorly given, this should be reflected in the rider's mark at the end of the test. Although, in each movement, the horse is marked for what he is doing, this is only a result of how or what he has been asked. Sometimes, you will feel a lot of sympathy for a horse apparently trying genuinely to do his job in spite of his rider! Unfortunately, you cannot allow this to sway your judgement, except that you might possibly put more blame on the rider than on the level of submission.

Whatever happens, all judges wish to see horse and rider working in harmony. They do not want a robotic performance, with total obedience but no 'life'. Everyone should bear in mind the object of dressage, which is to harness all the horse's natural abilities into a co-operative arrangement with the rider, neither being suppressed nor intimidated, but working together, united in enjoyment.

OBEDIENCE AND SUBMISSION

The Trainer

Without obedience to the rider's aids, submission to them cannot be achieved: obedience means instant acceptance of any given demand. Your job should be to ensure that the demands made by the rider are clear, and conveyed in such a way that the horse is able to give the response. The rider's seat should be well established, his aids positive and well co-ordinated. The horse's understanding of his rider's wishes can only develop gradually, as the repeat-and-reward process of training is built up.

To obtain obedience from the horse, you first need the pupil's respect so that he will want to do as you say. If a *rider* will accept mentally the necessity to obey, he will be better able to pass this on to his horse. He will expect to train his horse by correction and praise and you should help him to find the way to do this. Correction will sometimes seem harsh, but firm handling may be necessary in order to make a point.

You will be responsible for explaining the difference between fair punishment and cruelty. Your knowledge of how to treat a horse fairly will be crucial to success. You may have discovered from bitter experience that obtaining obedience is best gained through co-operation, not suppression. It is very sad to see a horse cowed or tense, because he has been frightened into obedience. This is not necessary, and only a happy horse working in unity with his rider will give the kind of performance that we all want to see.

OBEDIENCE AND SUBMISSION

The Rider

If you are going to be a successful competition rider, you will require a high standard of discipline from your horse. In addition, it is most important to realise the necessity for self-discipline. Before making an attempt to train the horse, you must be able to control your own physical and emotional reactions to a variety of situations.

You should also be prepared to get fit enough to do the job! This may involve riding several horses every day to build and strengthen the muscular system. It is no use trying to ride unless you do this, because you will be ineffective and become exhausted far too quickly. Strength will develop gradually as the various parts of your body adapt to the job they have to do.

Learning to sit well and maintain position is essential and you will need constant correction to avoid bad habits developing. Knowledge is crucial to your ability to be able to discipline the horse at the right moment and in such a way that it is understood. Do not miss any opportunity to learn.

The giving of aids that are correct, consistent and acceptable to the horse is a vital matter, which will need much practice and concentration. The horse, as we know, has an excellent memory. His learning relies on this, but he naturally retains both the good and the bad. His process of learning is from repetition and reward. Clearly, any instruction given to him must be correct and consistent, if his answer is also to be

Fitness may involve riding several horses a day.

correct and consistent. Only after having repeated an exercise correctly can a reward be given. This reward can be a pat on the neck or praise from the voice. Occasionally, the horse appears to defy an aid, or he may deliberately resist an order. This defiance should be dealt with firmly, sometimes even by a short punishment from the whip, followed by another try.

Sometimes, however sound your training may be, a misunderstanding can take place. This is not a serious fault. Careful thought on your part should determine whether it requires a firm correction or simply another attempt.

Horses are more likely to be obedient if they have had the opportunity to develop a relationship with the rider, built over a period of time, through the recognised communication system of the aids. Patience combined with firm correction should be your maxim, but you should only expect obedience if you build on a base of gradual understanding and physical development.

EVASIONS AND
RESISTANCES

The Judge

There are a great many ways in which, at times, the horse tries to evade the aids or puts up an objection to a particular move-. ment. Some evasions are: tilting or tipping the head; crossing the jaw; drawing the tongue back; putting it over the bit, hanging it out of the side of the mouth, putting it between the teeth; 'dropping' or coming 'behind the bit'; hanging the mouth open; overbending; going too deep.

It would be difficult to separate an evasion from a resistance except that the former is generally a passive avoidance whereas the latter is an obvious and active objection. By this, I refer to actions such as ears back, napping, kicking in response to the leg aids, coming 'above the bit', swinging the hindquarters, tail swishing and spooking, which some horses learn to use very successfully. Clearly, whether you define the problem as an evasion or a resistance, both remain unacceptable.

You may decide, in the case of an evasion, that the cause could be the bit or bits or the fitting of the bridle, in which case a helpful comment to this effect at the end of the test may be of use to the rider. There may, of course, be other causes, such as the rider's use of aids and spurs, or the background training.

Resistances, I think, emanate especially from hurried or incorrect training or a poor position or use of aids by the rider. This, in my view, is extremely serious, as a horse performing calmly and confidently in unison with his rider is a fundamental criterion of dressage. Therefore, any test that contains anxiety,

92

tension or resistance would be of little value.

Your calculation of the marks to award can only be made by considering the degree of evasion or resistance. In the case of tail swishing, for instance, it is necessary to gauge whether it is done through tension or in anger. In either case, this would deserve a lower mark than tail movement which is chiefly responding to the leg aids.

Also, resistance can be short-lived, for example being 'against the hand' in a transition. Again, you should decide whether this was caused by poor preparation on the part of the rider or some fault in the training. Your assessment would generally be based on the frequency of the problem.

You will often see 'unsteadiness', which could be construed as a resistance. More often than not, the blame can be attached to the rider for inconsistent or intermittent aids, but some unsteadiness can result from one-sidedness or stiffness; not, of themselves, resistance. This occurs a great deal in lower level tests and a careful assessment of the cause is important.

Obvious bit evasions or active resistance to the aids is more easily recognised than passive resistance which is harder to spot. In the latter there may be nothing apparent going wrong but the picture is not right. There is often a general air of unwillingness, a lack of fluidity. There is possibly tension in the horse's back and/or a setting of the mouth or poll. Many horses work in this way, their riders generally unaware that there is a problem because they have never ridden a supple submissive horse. Whatever the reason, this kind of resistance should be noted and marks given accordingly.

Any actual disobedience by the horse should be dealt with severely because, as already pointed out, one of the basic objects is for rider and horse to work harmoniously together. All problems emanating from incorrect acceptance of the bit should also be marked with resolution, as only with true sub-mission to the rider will the horse have any real future.

If you are a rider as well as a judge, and have experienced these problems yourself, you will be more aware of the various resistances and evasions that arise during training, and which are more easily corrected than others. This understanding is crucial to those you judge, in order that you place the right emphasis on those faults that are going to affect future progress.

EVASIONS AND RESISTANCES

The Trainer

Overcoming problems of evasion and resistance requires a twofold approach; dealing with those that occur during daily training at home, and those that crop up in the arena. Coping with difficulties at home is a much simpler task than trying to deal with them in a competition where, in addition to the judges, hundreds of people may be watching. You may have the task of advising your pupils how best to respond to all manner of problems so as not to 'blow' the test by over- or under-correction. Also, they must know when to *insist*, as a matter of principle, in order that the horse learns he cannot get away with being disobedient.

You will also have to advise on how and when to cover up a mistake which, even if still noticed by the discerning judge, might lose a mark less than if it is ignored. Some horses become ring-crafty, knowing that the rider is more at their mercy than when at home. Whatever the trouble, you must know about all the ways a horse finds to evade what he is asked, and how to prevent any active resistance.

Prevention being always more satisfactory than cure, you should try to teach horses and riders mainly along classical lines, laying a solid foundation upon which to build a sound step-by-step construction. Within this framework there should be a mutual trust, which helps a rider through times of trouble. If the framework is shaky and insecure, it may all fall apart at the crucial moment.

Many evasions stem from poor preparation for an exercise.

94

The horse, finding himself in an uncomfortable or physically difficult position, or not fully understanding his rider, may look for an easy way to save himself. He may find ways to avoid tongue pressure or discomfort from the bit, acceptance of the rider's collecting aids, or allowing himself to be suppled. He may tip or tilt his head, put his tongue over the bit or out of the mouth, or draw it back. He may drop the bit, overbend or try to be idle, to mention but a few.

There will also be more violent methods of resistance such as pulling, coming 'above the bit', napping, shying, kicking in response to aids, tail swishing, throwing his weight about and so on. Most resistance arises out of lack of harmony between horse and rider, either because the rider has not warned the horse properly of his intentions, or because he did not have the horse properly on the aids. Make certain, therefore, that the rider knows what he has to do and feels confident that the horse has understood the work. He should then be able to prevent all these faults or, if they do arise, to deal with them by checking on all fundamentals.

In the arena, the bond built up between horse and rider will assist the latter in knowing how to make a recovery, or what action to take, depending on the individual horse's temperament.

There will also be more violent methods of resistance.

EVASIONS AND RESISTANCES

The Rider

Training horses, it could be said, entails one long round of causing and overcoming evasions and resistances. Most problems could be avoided if approached with enough knowledge of the aim and how to get there but, unfortunately, few are so talented. Thus it is inevitable that we, as riders, cause most of our own setbacks, but those who succeed are the ones who are not deterred by difficulty or failure, but are resolved to overcome all.

Horses, naturally, do not necessarily wish to oblige us. More often than not, they would prefer to be out rolling in the paddock! It is, I think, asking a lot of them to accept to us riding them and, most especially, to accept the rigours of dressage. I do believe that it is important to understand this and make allowances by generally sympathetic handling of any situation.

With great patience and a gradual introduction to all new exercises, errors can be minimised. If you begin to encounter argument or dissent, you should carefully take stock, deciding whether you approached the subject too hastily and with too little preparation, or whether your base was not as secure as you thought. Knowledge of the fundamentals and how and when to go on are all part of learning, as is dealing with each problem as it arises.

Putting yourself in the horse's place may help in getting through the bad times but, even if you are the most sensitive rider in the world, you will have to learn when to be firm.

Putting yourself in the horse's position will sometimes do the trick.

Neither you nor the horse will enjoy the struggle. You will have to learn how to insist on what you want, when to persevere and when to ease up. Sometimes it will be a battle, but if you are committed, you will remain resolute, which in itself will help you to find the way. Do not misinterpret this advice and go 'looking for a fight' with the horse, or his various problems may well multiply. Instead, look for logical answers and apply skill, persistence and ingenuity to remove the horse's objections. Also, if you do have an argument and come through it, do make sure you praise the horse, so that next time you school him he will come out of the stable with eagerness, not dread.

ON THE FOREHAND

The Judge

Throughout your judging career you will see many horses on the forehand, especially in the lower level tests. Your calculation of the degree to which the horse's shoulders are taking the weight will dictate your ultimate judgement, and therefore the mark. It is inevitable that some horses will show poorer balance than others, either because their riders are ignorant or because they are unable to do anything about it. I would not suggest for a moment that these riders should be too harshly marked but, at the same time, I do recommend that judges should place a great deal of emphasis on this point. Overall balance is so crucial to any success at any level and, if horses are allowed to take too much weight on the forehand at the novice stage, they may never get off it! We are always pondering why there are so many promising horses starting in competition who never seem to get any further. I do believe that this is one of the main reasons, and judges can help by pointing it out.

I have heard the argument that event horses are more on the forehand than dressage horses at the same level because they have to gallop as well. Personally, I think this is nonsense. No horse should ever be on the forehand if ridden properly; it is the greatest hindrance to its performance in any sphere. I think that, as judges, we owe it to horses to encourage their riders to understand the importance of correct balance, and we should give marks accordingly.

ON THE FOREHAND

The Trainer

You will, I hope, be fully aware that a major part of dressage training is to transfer weight gradually from the forehand to the hindquarters, in order that the horse becomes balanced and thus able to do his work with greater ease.

In the ultimate stage, Grand Prix, the horse is required to work with lowered hindquarters, with his hind legs working actively well under his body, in order to be able to perform maximum collection and extension. Therefore it is of paramount importance that, as a trainer, you encourage this necessity at every stage. You must be aware of the horse's balance at all times and be able to help the rider to make improvements. At the lower levels there will, of course, be moments when it is less easy than others to achieve good balance. This is inevitable, but the biggest mistake is to encourage pupils to compete before a reasonable degree of balance is achieved. Almost certainly, under the stresses of competition, training will emerge below par. Unless this essential ingredient is well established the test may become a running battle, as neither horse nor rider can cope adequately with the demands made upon them.

There is, I think, a grave misunderstanding between the concept of working a horse in a low outline, allowing him to round his back and reach for the bit, and a horse who has all his weight on his shoulders. Make sure that you are clear on this point. A rider should be able to put the horse's head where he wants, but there is no need for the horse to be on the forehand.

ON THE FOREHAND

The Rider

The main feeling you will have with this problem is that the horse will feel heavy in front, may lean on your hands, or pull, or all three. You may also experience difficulty in manoeuvring in a small space or performing movements. The horse may feel stiff and awkward going round corners or circles, and his steps could feel uneven and lose rhythm. He could be difficult to control, especially in downward transitions. Both he and you may find the work exhausting.

Improving balance is the key to correction and, only if this quality is properly established at the start of training, can you be confident that it will not recur later on. Many movements can cause loss of balance but, if you have reached quite a high level of work or have been competing for some time, you should not be getting this comment.

Awareness of where the horse's weight is can give you the clue but, unless you focus your mind towards this point, you may not realise what is going on.

Novice horses may start off on the forehand, but should not remain there if properly ridden. Your job is first to train them gradually to equalise the weight over their four legs and then, as they learn more about engagement and collection, to transfer even more weight onto their hindquarters. The horse should not be pulled into this position, but should arrive at it from activity, suppleness and acceptance of the aids. He must learn not to rely on the hands for support but to carry himself, which he can only do in the right balance.

A clear picture of a horse taking too much weight on his forehand.

Sometimes, you may wish to work him low in order to stretch and round his back and allow freedom of the neck and head but, when doing so, you should still expect him to retain balance. If you get it right, it will be easy to trot or canter in the same speed and rhythm and to collect again without a struggle. If the horse falls onto his forehand when you give the rein he will feel a 'downhill' ride, may break the gait and will be difficult to 'bring together' again.

A good test of balance is the exercise of giving and re-taking the reins, which should be incorporated into all the work in order to find out whether the horse is carrying himself correctly.

101

CROUP HIGH

The Judge

There may be two main causes of this defect; the horse's conformation or poor training. Naturally, while you are judging a test, it is not your primary task to appraise conformation, but it may nevertheless account for the failure of the horse to lower his hindquarters as he should. Other than that, any horse who shows a tendency to raise his croup rather than lower it is proving that he is not being trained in the right way.

Ultimate success in Grand Prix derives from an ability on the horse's part to take weight onto the hindquarters whilst remaining in a rounded outline, supple and submissive. If horses are not encouraged to do this both by correct training and sound judging, they will not reach such heights. I suggest, therefore, that a firm view be taken of this flaw. This is especially applicable to any collected work or transitions where it is essential to develop the principle. If you fail to notice this fault and reward the performance incorrectly the rider may well be left unaware that there is a problem. Later in the training where greater lowering of the hindquarters is required the rider will really come unstuck, which will be a great disappointment after early success. This applies in general of course, but this particular fault will prevent attainment of a high mark especially in canter pirouettes, piaffe and passage where the lightness of the forehand is critical.

In addition, it is important to understand that if the horse is going croup high his back is also affected as the croup cannot be raised without tension, which of course is incorrect.

CROUP HIGH

The Trainer

It is advisable to avoid buying a horse for dressage who is built croup high. The job is difficult enough without taking on a physical problem such as this. One of your chief tasks throughout the many months and years of training will be to teach the horse to lower his hindquarters. Some horses naturally find this easy, others do not. A horse who does not may raise his objection by stiffening his back in order to avoid bringing his hind legs under his body. This tension can develop into an active resistance against the lowering of the croup, and manifests itself in a disunited way of going, with choppy, un-rhythmic gaits. If these flaws are not eradicated, the horse will have great difficulty in canter pirouettes, piaffe and passage – high earners of marks in the Grand Prix. At a lower level, canter work is especially vulnerable, with the horse taking short, tense strides – possibly in four-time and hollow in outline.

Should you notice any tendency in this direction, it is advisable to return to basics. The horse must be brought on throughout his training in a rounded outline, being encouraged to engage his hind legs under his body. Only through perseverance can this become an established way of going which can be maintained through all movements.

CROUP HIGH
The Rider

Your ability to recognise this defect will stem from the feeling you have of the reaction to your leg aids and the action of the horse's back beneath your seat.

If, when you apply the leg aids, you feel an immediate 'tucking under' of the horse's hind legs which takes you forwards, this would indicate a correct reaction. If, on the other hand, you get a sluggish response, the reaction may be unsatisfactory. This, of itself, would not necessarily make the croup come up, but it may not have lowered either – an essential feature of the correct response.

Regarding the back, this should be rounding, which will give a feeling of vibrance and softness to sit on. If it is hard and unyielding it will be uncomfortable and, although this may not actually bring up the croup, it is tension and stiffness which can start the fault off. Any feeling of the horse taking most of his weight on his shoulders could certainly allow the fault to develop. This particularly applies to canter, which is the gait most at risk. This can give a very unbalanced feeling, with the horse soon becoming hollow in outline and losing the correct three-beat rhythm. As you can see, this would be disastrous for the whole future training and many marks could be lost in tests.

When you reach the stage of teaching the horse piaffe, it will be essential that the hindquarters come under him to lift the forehand. If you feel that the shoulders are dropping or the steps are not lifting it may be that the horse is tending to become croup high. Rather than persevere with that movement, do ride forwards out of it and do some work on your half-halts, making certain that you are performing them properly with the hind legs under the horse. This correction applies to all other movements as well.

This picture shows the engaged hindquarters lifting the forehand.

'ABOVE THE BIT'

The Judge

Recognition of this fault can be developed by taking an imaginary horizontal line through the horse from nose to tail, level with the horse's back. If his nose is above this line he will in all probability be hollow along his topline, and also be 'above the bit'. If he performs in this shape he will inevitably develop incorrect musculature and may, in addition, suffer strain. Because the weight of the rider will add to the problem, work becomes awkward for the horse, making him reluctant or unable to co-operate.

The cause of the problem derives from three main factors. The first is lack of knowledge, 'feel' or awareness on the rider's part. This deficiency will allow or even encourage the horse to respond incorrectly, depending upon the aids given. A rider who is lacking in 'feel' will be unable to make the necessary corrections, and may not even know that they are needed.

The second cause of the horse coming 'above the bit' is likely to be poor training. If the rider has understood and followed a progressive system of training, he will have realised the importance of the basic principles, one of which is to work the horse in a rounded outline. If he has failed to grasp this criterion sufficiently, or has been impatient or hasty, then this fault could be the result.

The third cause is somewhat less significant than the other two as it is when there is a momentary coming 'above the bit' or hollowing resulting from a hurried aid, lack of preparation, loss of balance or even a rough piece of ground. Provided that the outline is correct prior to and following the moment of hollowness, then it should not be marked harshly. If it is sustained, or recurs frequently, then clearly a more serious view should be taken. Any hollowing of the back, even without active resistance, will prevent the horse from being able to engage his hind legs, and promotes stiffness rather than suppleness.

Horses who are habitually 'above the bit' are seen more frequently at the lower levels of competition, when both rider and horse are learning. I do not believe that undue leniency should be shown to this. The truth is that, unless the rider realises his mistake and puts it right, his horse's whole training will be affected. Many good horses are spoilt in the early stages and I think that judges have to take the initiative to make it clear where the rider is going wrong. This is especially important when, as with this particular fault, the horse will suffer — being unable to perform correctly and probably showing much resistance as a result.

Momentary hollowing may be viewed more kindly at the lower levels but, as the difficulty of the exercises increases, so the correct shape becomes more and more important, in which case strict observance of it should be made.

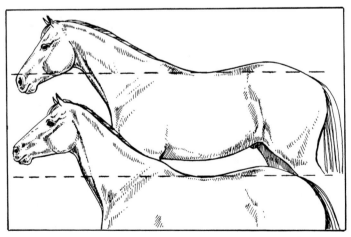

If a horse's nose is above an imaginary line drawn
through the horse from nose to tail, level with the back,
he will probably be hollow along his topline
and 'above the bit'.

'ABOVE THE BIT'

The Trainer

It is essential to accept that this problem is a very serious fault. Any horse, if allowed to work repeatedly 'above the bit' or with a hollow back, is not only going to find the work exceedingly difficult but may actually suffer physical harm. If this point is accepted then pupils should be taught early on how to achieve a rounded outline. This should come as a result of engagement, suppleness and acceptance of the bit. Clearly, the horse should understand the aids, which must be given in a precise and consistent manner. However, one must also accept that there are times when there will be misunderstandings, or actual resistance to the rider. Regarding the former, it is your job to prepare both parties sufficiently well to ensure that problems do not arise too often. In cases of resistance, you will discover through experience of dealing with horses of varying temperament and abilities how to correct them.

In tests, many marks will be lost if the horse is 'above the bit' or goes hollow, even if only for a moment but, if you have followed a systematic training programme, with gradual development towards the goal, you should usually be able to avoid any real difficulty. If your pupils are being criticised for this fault in Advanced Level tests, you have failed badly and should review your methods.

Sometimes, you will be asked to re-train a horse who has been brought on in the wrong way and either resists when asked to go 'on the bit' or has become so stiff that he is almost unable to round his back. However for the horse who has managed to progress, there is really only one thing to do, and this is to go back to the beginning and re-form the essentials. Such horses may need to be worked with their heads 'on the floor' for a while until their tensions are reduced but, although this decision may be made, it should be understood that no weight should be allowed onto the shoulders because of it. Good balance will be all-important to the ultimate improvement.

As the rider has collected the horse he has hollowed and his neck has come too high and drawn back.

'ABOVE THE BIT'

The Rider

You will feel that your horse is going like this in two main ways: his head will seem to be up in the air, and he will be difficult to control. Other factors may also be apparent. His neck, instead of arching over the crest, may flatten or hollow and his poll may be very high, with his nose pointing out in front of him. Sometimes, when the condition is very exaggerated, you may even be able to see part of his forehead.

With his head in this position he will also, inevitably, have a hollow back. This you will feel because it is like 'sitting in a dish'. Two things result from this; first, the aids cannot be effective and second, both the horse's mouth and back will feel hard and unyielding.

In order to work properly beneath the rider it is necessary for the horse to be in a rounded outline. This way he can engage his hind legs under his body, can use himself in an elastic manner and may be controlled by the aids. Only from a complete understanding of this fact will any rider achieve his aim. In tests, many marks may be lost for even momentary hollowing or coming 'above the bit' and although, at the lower levels, it may be viewed more leniently, in the higher ones it most certainly will not.

Of course, no-one is perfect and there may be an occasional lapse. Generally, these lapses occur during a movement when perhaps insufficient preparation was made. The horse may have lost impulsion or become too strong, or perhaps a specific bend was not taken in time. If you can recover quickly, then only a mark or two may be lost. If the overall training has been correct, then this recovery is possible; if not, then you will be in deep trouble.

Even the best-trained horses sometimes let you down!

'BEHIND THE BIT'

The Judge

This state exists when the horse refuses to go forwards into the rein contact but sits just behind it, avoiding the pressure. He may or may not be overbent but will almost certainly have drawn back his neck. Because he is not at that moment 'on the aids', control will be erratic and the rider may have trouble in really going forwards. This can apply particularly in piaffe where it is relatively easy to drop forward inclination and impulsion. Walk and rein-back are also movements where it can easily occur. In trot or canter, the horse would be more likely to be overbent or going deep, with the poll lowered and a break in the outline of the neck.

Sometimes the tongue will come over the bit, at others the tongue may be drawn back. In either case, the horse is making it easy for himself to avoid the pressure of the bit or bits. It should be relatively easy to observe these two evasions, especially since there will probably be a good deal of resistance by the horse, combined with an open mouth. If the horse is not actively evading the rider, the fault may be seen only by the amount of tension on the reins. If the reins tend to be slack or loose, the horse may be 'behind the bit'. This latter assessment should be made with great care, as it may simply be that the rider has not taken up the slack. With experience however, the difference between the horse 'dropping the bit' himself and the rider loosening the contact will become obvious.

The marking of this defect should depend on its degree and whether it is continuous or intermittent. Bearing in mind that

112

correct acceptance of the aids is one of the basic essentials, a careful calculation should be made and, without being too harsh, a firm stand taken. It is not easy, however, to define precisely what impact this evasion should have on the marks given, as much also depends on the horse's state of mind. Often, a horse comes 'behind the bit' through anxiety, not simply to avoid pain or discomfort – although these may be contributory factors. The rider's application of aids and sympathy in overcoming the problem may be taken into account in the rider mark at the end of the test.

The horse obviously dislikes his rider's aids at the moment.

'BEHIND THE BIT'

The Trainer

When you are faced with this problem, the first thing to do is to seek the cause. This may be to do with the bitting of the horse causing discomfort; a careful appraisal should be made. If you are satisfied that this is not the reason, next observe the rider's aids. These may lack co-ordination or sympathy, either of which may make the horse seek an evasion. If, once the aids have been checked, the situation does not improve, the method of training should be investigated!

If the work has been systematic, the horse being brought along in a gradual manner, any deficiencies of this kind should be spotted and dealt with on the way. If, on the other hand, the training has been hurried or short cuts attempted, the horse may learn to save himself by using this evasion. Once he has learnt that it is possible to avoid pressure on his mouth by coming 'behind the bit' or 'dropping the bit', he may do so more and more frequently.

Anxiety can be the trigger, because any tension causes a horse to search for ways to avoid being pressured. It is therefore most important that a calm attitude and sympathetic approach to all work is preserved.

However good a trainer you may be, it would be unrealistic not to acknowledge that certain horses may, at sometime in their training, become anxious and discover this particular evasion. This could occur especially during piaffe or rein-back, where there is little or no forward movement. This, however, is the crux of the issue, as if forward inclination is carefully

114

maintained and combined with the co-ordinated and sensitive use of the aids, the horse will have little or no opportunity or desire to evade. Of course, mistakes will be made so, if the evasion develops, time should be spent on restoring confidence and encouraging the horse once more to 'seek the bit'. A loose rein will not achieve this result. Only by riding forwards with a firm leg into a contact which allows the horse to stretch his neck and bring his nose in front of the vertical will an answer be found. Any sign of a repeat of the evasion should be dealt with in this way. The pupil's greater understanding of the half-halt and its correct execution will also help in overcoming this problem.

Ride forwards with a firm leg contact which encourages the horse to bring his nose in front of the vertical.

115

'BEHIND THE BIT'

The Rider

It is not always easy for the less experienced rider to know when the horse is 'behind the bit'. In dressage, the rider should always be seeking a lightness of the forehand and with it, a light feeling in the hands from a yielding to the bit. Sometimes the horse responds in the right way but, at others, he may *feel* light when he has, in fact, simply 'dropped the bit'. Because there is no great weight in the hands to contend with, this may give a feeling of elation to the rider but, if the horse has indeed 'dropped the bit' – or 'come behind it' – he will be increasingly awkward to manoeuvre as the important connection between his front and back ends will be missing. There could also be a feeling of being 'stuck' in a particular gait or variant because, without real control in the horse's mouth, it becomes impossible to ask anything constructive with the legs.

Dressage training requires that the horse responds to co-ordinated use of the aids. He should show a desire to go forwards, yet allow himself to be flexed by the rider, and permit precise control. This cannot take place if he is not accepting the bit, so many marks can be lost in a test.

If you believe that your horse has learned the trick of coming 'behind the bit' in order to evade your aids, I advise that you first check the bridle. Make sure that the bit(s) is/are correctly fitted and then have a good look at your own aids. If these points are in order, you can then begin to correct the evasion by sending the horse more forwards. Do not let him rush out of rhythm or balance, but do try to use correct half-halts to ensure that these points are not changeable. As you ride forwards, be ready to allow the horse freedom to stretch his neck and reach for the bit. This does not mean giving the rein contact away — in fact it is most important not to do this — but your arms and hands should allow any desire by the horse to take his nose forwards. You may find that he is very reluctant to do this and it can take a lot of time and patience to achieve it. In fact it may be necessary to use alternate flexions which will cause the horse to have to accept pressure on one side of his mouth and then the other. This should induce a gradual acceptance. He will be less able to 'sit behind' the bit if he is made to feel it in this way.

As you ride forwards, be ready to allow the horse freedom to stretch his neck.

The horse may have developed this fault because of worry over some particular exercise. Try to deduce whether this could be the case. If so, then part of the correction will involve obtaining calmness and better harmony between the two of you. In all the exercises that you attempt, a forward inclination is desirable. Try to ensure that you do not put yourself or the horse in a position where this quality has been lost, as it is at such a moment that you could be inviting this evasion to develop.

As well as dropping the bit some horses learn that if they roll back their tongues they can evade pressure in that way. This can be very difficult indeed to correct as there is no real physical means of doing so. Artificial methods are not a cure. Only by going back to basics will there be a chance of correction and this may depend on the age of the horse. If the horse has habitually used this evasion for a long period it may not be possible to eliminate it. The only way to make a lasting improvement is to teach the horse better acceptance of the aids in general and prevent him becoming worked up as this may well start up the habit again.

During training it is always important to recognise quickly when something is going wrong. It is not easy to feel when the horse has come 'behind the bit', nor whether he is doing something with his tongue that he should not do. Experience will provide answers but of course having the advice of a trainer or judge, if you know one well enough to ask, can be a great help. All evasions are troublesome but if this one develops it is a particular nuisance.

PART FIVE
Basic Essentials

Without correct engagement or sufficient impulsion, the quality of work will be seriously affected.

ENGAGEMENT AND IMPULSION

The Judge

Only by continuous study of a subject, with a full understanding of the principles involved, will you be able to judge it satisfactorily.

Without correct engagement or sufficient impulsion the quality of the horse's work will be seriously affected. You will constantly be required to see whether those qualities have been lost, causing many things to go wrong. Without sufficient engagement, the horse will not be in a position to balance and carry himself, so he may perform much of the work on the forehand. In this position, he will probably be unable to maintain rhythm and regularity within the gaits, and will be unable to collect or extend adequately. His lateral work will be affected and he will labour. He will be unable to perform canter pirouettes properly, or to do flying changes, piaffe or passage expressively. Without lowered hindquarters, all the transitions will be a problem as his weight tips forward and downward onto his rider's hands. Whenever the horse finds something difficult, he may use resistance to express the struggle he is encountering. The rider is clearly at fault for placing the horse in this situation, and this should be taken into account in the rider mark at the end of the test.

Similarly, without impulsion, the horse cannot perform the movements properly. There is still a misconception on the part of some less experienced judges, who confuse impulsion with speed. Naturally, the horse should be made to go forwards with plenty of energy, but this energy, having been encouraged

121

by the rider, should also be contained by him. Containing impulsion should not be confused with restriction, where the rider prevents the horse from going forwards freely. True containment is control over the amount of energy which takes the horse forwards at a given moment, together with constant adjustment of the degree of energy. Each movement requires its own degree of energy and you should be able to assess this. Insufficient impulsion will affect the quality of the steps, especially their spring, precision and size. Without sufficient energy the horse will lack the moment of suspension which he should show in trot and canter. Impulsion should give a performance 'life'. There is nothing worse than seeing a dull, 'wooden' display.

A horse full of impulsion really covering the ground.

ENGAGEMENT AND IMPULSION

The Trainer

Even if you thoroughly understand the principles, this subject is not easy to teach either horse or rider.

ENGAGEMENT

The Horse

It may be advantageous to both horse and pupil if you are able to ride the horse to teach him how to accept being engaged! So much resistance can evolve from the procedure of 'bringing the horse together'. He first has to learn to answer a light leg aid immediately it is applied. Having done so and gone forward he is then sometimes baffled by the extra control being taken by the rider's hands. This control should not, of course, be restrictive, but carefully regulated, never allowing the horse to feel trapped or unable to go forwards. He must respond by yielding to the bit. Only if he is sufficiently supple through his body will the result of the engagement be really effective. You will find, when seeking to achieve satisfactory engagement, that work on lateral exercises (see page 193) and transitions using half-halts (see page 167) will bring the horse gradually towards the ultimate. This will be piaffe, passage and canter pirouettes – where a real lowering of the hindquarters is necessary so that the horse can support his own weight and that of his rider in the right balance.

123

The Rider

If the horse understands what he has to do it will be easier for the rider to grasp, as your setting up the horse will make the feeling clearer. Co-ordination of the aids is the key to success. Some riders have natural co-ordination, others find it all very difficult. Your job will be to discover how best to put this co-ordination across without constantly having to 'ride the horse from the ground'! This may be necessary for quite some time, until each movement is felt and understood. Obviously, the rider's position in the saddle will affect the influence of the aids. Constant correction to the way the rider sits and how the aids are applied should be given, together with instructions on strength of contact of leg and hand. Eventually, the horse will permit himself to be 'brought together' without resistance, while the rider, developing his sense of anticipation for what can go wrong, will be able to prevent problems rather than having to correct them.

IMPULSION

The Horse

Going hand in glove with the engagement of the hindquarters is the energy being built up in them. As the horse is able to support himself more through his hindquarters taking more weight, so any increased activity requested by the rider will produce the power which generates forward momentum. It is this that the horse needs to perform all movements properly, and that the rider has to control. From the horse's point of view, he has to learn to accept that control. This is not always easy for him, because a lot of energy, misapplied, very easily destroys the balance. Balance is essential to the ease with which the horse can perform, and to the purity of the gaits. Loss of balance will cause difficulties and may result in resistance. To balance with energy (impulsion) is a long-term affair and is part of the process of systematic training.

The Rider

Teaching the rider to obtain impulsion and control it will also take some time. Once the rider understands how to ask for engagement he will then be in a position to bring about varying degrees of impulsion. He will certainly need your assistance in learning what degree is necessary at each stage of training, and in discovering how to control it without restricting the horse's movement. So often you will find that a pupil, having asked for more energy will, through lack of knowledge or 'feel', prevent that energy from doing what he had wanted it to do. Only from a correct, secure seat and use of aids will it all be possible, so constant advice and correction on this aspect is important.

If the horse is unwilling to give the rider what is being asked for, the rider must use a schooling whip as an additional aid. Many riders are ineffective in this department. Some are not firm enough; others will use the whip too harshly, which only disturbs whatever has already been achieved. If the whip destroys the rhythm or balance, resultant resistances will hinder progress. Teaching pupils to use a whip to good effect is important. Without it, aids may never be adequately refined. There is nothing worse than watching a rider 'kick up' the whole time, and it must be unpleasant for the horse as well.

In order to instruct your pupils accordingly, you must be very clear about the degree of impulsion acceptable to the judges at varying levels. In an ideal world, your ideas on the subject would coincide with judges, but if they do not, it is foolish to be stubborn if you want pupils to win. In competition, compromises do sometimes have to be made. Some judges prefer to see a relaxed performance with less impulsion, while others mark up those who really 'go some-where'. Naturally you would believe that the latter, without tension or resistance, is your aim. Provided both entities can achieve this it should, on the whole, put your pupils 'in the frame'.

Riders and judges do frequently mistake speed for impulsion. Do not compromise on this aspect. Speed can prevent the horse from becoming properly impulsive because he is racing forwards onto his forehand. True, useful impulsion, as has been explained, is dependent on the correct engagement of the hindquarters to lift the forehand – something which cannot be done if the horse is 'running'. It is a very different matter accepting less impulsion in a good balance than a travesty of

Riders often mistake speed for impulsion.

too much in the wrong balance. The former can be worked on but, with the latter, you have to begin again.

CORRECTNESS OF GAITS

As with everything you do in training, the correctness of the gaits is paramount. Watch constantly for any deficiencies which may creep in as a result of too little or too much energy. A four-time canter, for example, can evolve very easily unless under constant scrutiny, as can an incorrect walk sequence such as pacing or being irregular (one leg taking a shorter step than another). In trot, 'dwelling' or 'running' are two common faults. Your knowledge of faults which may arise from pupils overriding or being ineffective will, clearly, enable you to give the right advice in this all-important matter.

ENGAGEMENT AND IMPULSION

The Rider

Without sufficient engagement or impulsion your horse will not be able to operate efficiently, much less will he be able to go through the rigours of a test, where movements follow one another so quickly.

ENGAGEMENT

To be able to go easily from one movement to the next the horse needs to be in excellent, sustainable balance. The engagement of the hindquarters is the first step towards such balance, as they are then in a position to lift and lighten the forehand.

How do you ask for engagement and how do you know when you have got it? Achieving it in the first place does depend upon an ability to feel when the horse is in natural balance, that is to say, not being supported by the reins. After that, the next step is to bring the horse together by means of co-ordinated aids, so that he learns to collect. If he submits to the aids he will begin to bring his hindquarters more under the body, and the hind legs will step further under as well. You should start to feel this happening; it will be combined with an increased feeling of activity of the hind legs, that is, a bending of the joints, accompanied by a feeling of lift.

Another clue is whether you can maintain a correct sequence

of steps in all gaits. Without engagement it will be hard to keep the steps in a regular rhythm so the sequence can suffer, especially in canter.

Engagement can only really take place if the horse's back is sufficiently supple and flexible to allow it, so you will need to work on lateral exercises during the development process.

IMPULSION

This is the forward energy which propels the horse along. Correct, useful impulsion is dependent upon the engagement of the hindquarters. A dressage horse is required to transfer weight onto his hindquarters so that he can carry himself forward energetically in a balance that will enable him to move freely with a light forehand. True impulsion is when the energy produced by the horse's hindquarters travels through his body, uninterrupted by stiffness, resistance or restriction by the rider, and takes him forwards.

How do you know whether or not you have sufficient impulsion? It is not always easy to tell, as different degrees of impulsion are acceptable at different levels of training. It may not be wise to over-simplify but, as a basis for recognition, you may ask yourself whether the horse is labouring through his work, or performing it with ease. If the answer is the former, you can be certain that you do not have sufficient impulsion. If this is the case, you must first make the horse respond more quickly and actively to your seat and leg aids. The schooling whip may be needed to achieve this, producing a greater desire to go forwards.

If it is to be used to effect, impulsion has to be contained, controlled and distributed in a way suitable for a particular movement. Only time and experience will really tell you how to achieve this. Impulsion is sometimes misplaced, that is to say, the horse may appear to be going forwards with great energy, but this could be detrimental if the correct sequences of the gaits are affected, or if irregular or unrhythmic steps develop. It can be very awkward for the horse if he is over-impulsed, especially at Novice and Elementary Levels, as he can easily lose balance, which may give rise to resistances. Also, he cannot cope with leg aids which drive him into a bit that he has not yet entirely learned to accept. There is also a danger of too much containing or restricting of impulsion which can, instead of taking the horse forwards, lift the steps higher than the natural lift (for example, the walk could take the appearance of a 'Spanish walk' as seen in a circus, or a passage-type trot may evolve).

Learning how to contain impulsion correctly will quite probably take a considerable time, depending on your natural ability to co-ordinate your aids and whether you can use a half-halt effectively.

True impulsion is uninterrupted by stiffness, resistance or restriction by the rider.

SUPPLENESS

The Judge

The FEI states that:

> The object of Dressage is the harmonious development of the physique and ability of the horse. As a result it makes the horse calm, supple, loose and flexible, but also confident, attentive and keen, thus achieving perfect understanding with his rider.

Therefore, at all levels of work you will want to see the horse uninhibited by tension or stiffness. Any part of the horse that may be in opposition to the rider or the movement being ridden can cause lack of freedom and flexibility. In the gaits, the steps will be affected by tension, which will prevent them from producing cadence and spring, and transitions and lateral movements will only be correct if the horse is supple. Without suppleness a test cannot be 'put together' fluently.

You will be looking for two sorts of suppleness. The first is the ability of the horse to flex longitudinally; to engage his hindquarters and move with a supple, rounded back. This can only come about if the horse accepts containment of his impulsion by the relaxation of his poll and lower jaw. The second variety is the flexibility of the horse laterally; his capacity to bend around the rider's inside leg and show freedom by optimum use of his limbs and shoulders.

SUPPLENESS

The Trainer

Much of the training will entail attending to this factor. Without it, the horse will be unable to perform the movements well enough; the rider will find the horse awkward to manoeuvre, making the test a laborious task.

Therefore, from the beginning, you should use exercises which will bring about muscular pliability. With a novice horse, such exercises are: circles of 20 or 15 m; half-circles; serpentines; loops; transitions; minor gait variations; half-halts and a degree of shoulder-in. These will bend the horse longitudinally and laterally, preparing him for the next stage, which is collection. Work on this aspect of training should bring more improvement, and enables the horse to show greater gait variation – which, in itself, is an aid to suppling.

The lateral exercises can then be introduced; also, with an able horse and knowledgable pupil, the start of piaffe, to aid further engagement of the hindquarters and provide a greater degree of activity and energy. Throughout the routine, strict attention should be given to submission, for without good acceptance of the aids true suppleness will not be attained.

Although a good deal of your attention will be necessarily focused on the horse, just as much emphasis should be placed on the rider, to make sure that, at all times, the horse's movement can be absorbed. A stiff rider will certainly make a stiff horse.

SUPPLENESS

The Rider

In this instance, we shall discuss the quality of suppleness primarily in the rider, rather than the horse. However, it should be understood that a rider will only be able to develop his own suppleness in conjunction with that of his horse. It is very difficult — well nigh impossible — to become supple yourself if the horse you are riding is rigid in his way of going.

First, it is important to have the correct concept of suppleness — being loose and flopping about it certainly is not!

Learning how to combine relaxation with muscles that can be used effectively will enable the body to be flexible and absorb the movement of the horse.

An ability to sit deep and maintain a correct classical position is the first essential. This can only be arrived at from training the seat to be close to the horse at all times. Riding without stirrups certainly helps, but only if the seat muscles relax sufficiently to allow maximum contact. Tension in the thigh or gripping with the knee or lower leg prevents this, and also prevents the leg muscles from influencing the horse in the right way.

The legs should be round the horse from hip to heel, held there in such a way that they correctly influence and allow every movement of the horse. Knees and toes which turn out cause tension in the joints and prevent the aids from being given as they should.

The upper body should be held upright, but not rigidly so; the loins should be pliable enough to absorb any movement which the horse makes. The shoulders must not droop, but should be held vertically over the seat to balance the position, a remark which applies also to the head.

The upper arms should rest against the upper body, with flexion at the elbows, the lower arms and hands being attached to the reins as though these were extensions of themselves. Any joint which is rigid will prevent elasticity, thereby spoiling the contact.

Training the body to work in the right way takes considerable time and requires a lot of effort and dedicated work, but without this accomplishment it will be hard to produce a harmonious performance.

This rider is demonstrating a very well-maintained position in an extended trot.

CIRCLES AND HALF-CIRCLES

The Judge

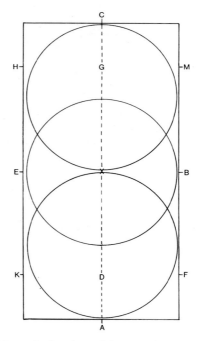

Circles of any size in any gait should retain the basic principles of that gait and the rounded outline of the horse should be steady, showing no resistance. The bend of the horse should always relate to the circle size; when the circles become smaller,

20 m circles in a 20 m × 40 m arena

greater collection and engagement are called for. Only a balanced, supple horse will be able to describe circles of varying size correctly, whilst maintaining regular, rhythmic steps.

You will certainly see circles of the wrong size, and these should not get a very high mark. Odd shapes should also be marked only moderately.

Unlevelness, showing that stiffness is present, is common and should be marked down. Incorrect bend should receive a low mark, as should any circles ridden with the horse on the forehand.

All the foregoing remarks apply also to half-circles, which should be accurate in extent.

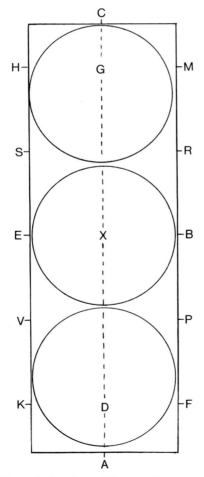

20 m circles in a 20 m × 60 m arena

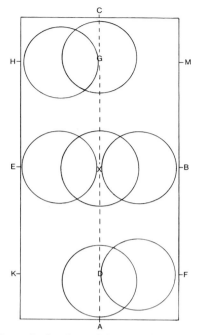

10 m circles in a 20 m × 40 m arena

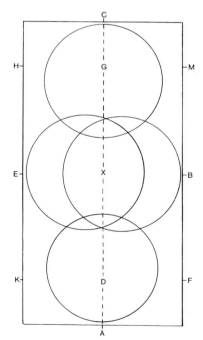

15 m circles in a 20 m × 40 m arena

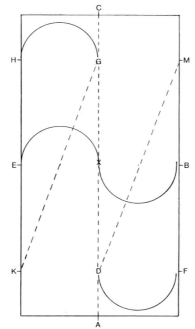

10 m half-circles in a 20 m × 40 m arena

CIRCLES

Riders are responsible for the shape and size of a circle. They should show that they are able to prepare the horse properly and should look where they are going. It will be evident whether they are sitting evenly or crooked and this will almost certainly affect the way a horse is going. This point should be mentioned in the rider mark. Some riders are habitually crooked and crookedness is one thing that can have such a detrimental influence on the horse. If a shoulder-in position has been taken, the horse will be balanced and upright in the circle. Any leaning in or deviation of the horse's outside shoulder, swinging of the hindquarters or excessive bend in the horse's neck, should be marked down.

HALF-CIRCLES

When a half-circle is followed by a return to the track the horse should be straight. When changing from one half-circle to another the change of bend should be gradual, smooth and free from resistance.

CIRCLES AND HALF-CIRCLES

The Trainer

Teaching the horse to perform circles or half-circles of any size is all a matter of introducing him to each specific bend, moulding him from the aids to the curve required. Circles or half-circles of less than 20 m diameter are simply a matter of progression. As the horse develops in engagement, so he will be able to maintain balance and regularity round smaller curves. At all times the hind feet should follow in the tracks of the forefeet. If the horse should flounder and become unlevel, or lose his rhythm, he may not be ready for an exercise of that difficulty. Smaller curves, in any case, should follow work on shoulder-in, which should have brought the horse to a stage where he is able to adopt more bend.

Do avoid putting too much emphasis on this subject early on in the training; it could put a strain on the horse which may be harmful.

Teaching the rider to judge sizes accurately and use the aids correctly is another task. Judging distance and size is a matter of practice and experience, but be fussy about making corrections, so that there is no chance of the figures becoming haphazard. However, unless the pupil is able to ride shoulder-in properly, he may struggle to keep appropriate bends. The rider must be able to control the horse adequately from the inside leg to the outside hand, with combined assistance as necessary from the other leg and hand and the seat.

CIRCLES AND HALF-CIRCLES

The Rider

Although there are many circles or half-circles of different sizes to ride in all gaits, you have two main concerns. The first is being able to take a bend in the first place and keep it, and the second is judging the size and shape correctly.

When you are learning about bend you will become aware of the absolute necessity of having obedient response to your inside leg aid. The horse must go forward from it and, if asked, move away from it. Controlling this reaction is the job of the outside hand, which receives the energy from your inside leg and regulates its distribution.

With your inside hand you should be asking for a flexion to the inside. This flexion is only sufficient to 'soften' the horse's mouth on that side and initiate the curve.

You should expect the hindquarters to respond to your outside leg by curving round your inside leg, but only as much as the specific curve of the line you are following. The hindquarters should always follow the forehand, and never be 'in' or 'out'.

You may find that the horse will try to evade the bend by leaning on his inside shoulder or escaping onto his outside one. It is important to be able to ride shoulder-in, as this will give you the control of the forehand and the bend and enable you to prepare the horse and make corrections.

Before you can attempt smaller curves you will need to teach the horse some collection, but this should, in any case, be evolving from riding shoulder-in.

Do watch out that you do not bend the horse's neck more

than the remainder of his body and that the engagement and impulsion are kept up.

Any hollowing of outline or unlevelness of steps is a sign that the horse is not ready for the size of curve you want. He will soon let you know through resistances that he is unhappy, but do take these warning signs to heart and reconsider the matter. Never allow the horse to labour through a movement, as it could harm him. You will find that you can only retain real momentum in all this work if the horse is going forward and is sufficiently supple.

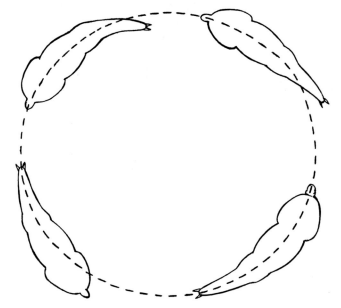

Common faults on the circle: (clockwise from bottom left) hindquarters out; neck overbent; neck underbent; correct.

SERPENTINES

The Judge

The FEI definition states:

> The serpentine consists of half-circles connected by a straight line. Depending on the size of the half-circles the straight connection varies in length.

IN TROT

In all trot serpentines you will want to see a supple and balanced horse, changing bend fluently, without resistance or loss of outline. Any discrepancies of the gait, unsteadiness or stiffness, should be firmly penalised.

Some less educated riders will ride serpentines with wrong bend or allow the horse to be 'above the bit'. This is, of course, very wrong and harmful to the horse. Although a judge is not there to teach, some helpful comment should be made in this instance.

IN CANTER

Serpentines in this gait, whether in true canter or counter-canter, should show the same qualities of balance and outline as trot except, of course, that the bend should be kept to the leading leg.

Sufficient engagement, collection and impulsion should be present to enable the horse to perform the movements as laid down. If changes of leg are involved – whether simple changes through walk or flying changes – the horse should show calmness, flexibility and obedience.

Although the number of walk steps in a simple change is not laid down, approximately three at higher levels and more earlier on is acceptable. The accent should be placed more on the transitions than on the number of steps.

In a serpentine where changes are involved, especially if they are from counter-canter to counter-canter, or true lead to counter-canter, good balance is imperative. An equal bend to each leg is also important.

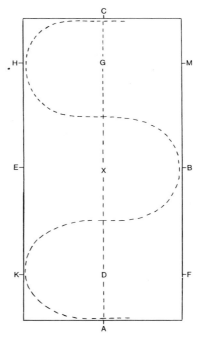

Three-loop serpentine in a 20 m × 40 m arena

SERPENTINES

The Trainer

When teaching serpentines to pupils you may have to give a demonstration and clear explanation of the various movements, in order to get over the details of the route to take. I find that the less knowledgeable get into an awful muddle otherwise. It is essential to get across the necessity of a gradual change of bend when performed in trot, with sufficient use of the aids to maintain balance and outline.

In canter, some novice riders even try to change the bend instead of keeping it to the leading leg. Many have difficulty in holding the flexion and also directing the horse. I personally allow novice riders to use the direct rein for direction, but only in so far as it brings the horse straight. As soon as they have grasped the use of their leg aids I make them also keep a flexion, however small.

Of course, no movement will be performed well unless the horse is engaged sufficiently and has enough impulsion. In the canter work on these exercises, collection is of vital importance. If the serpentine involves simple changes, it is the collection and maintenance of engagement that gives the rider the chance to make direct transitions.

In the case of a serpentine with flying changes, either true lead to counter-canter, or counter-canter to counter-canter, the collection and sustained engagement are critical. Although the bend to the leading leg should always be retained, it should not be so excessive as to hinder the capacity of the horse to change direction.

The position of the horse on the approach to the centre line is also a matter of prime importance. If he is not precisely balanced, the change and the departure from the line will be impaired. It is easier for the rider to 'go back on himself' slightly prior to the change, as this allows the change of bend more chance. Obtaining a change directly over the centre line is a matter of knowing each horse's stride and of teaching your pupils the necessary control.

An expressive and seemingly straight flying change.

SERPENTINES

The Rider

Serpentines can be quite puzzling to work out if you are unfamiliar with them. Also, they feel strange to ride unless your horse has done them before.

IN TROT

The first criterion is to be able to keep an active, balanced trot which is in a rhythm and 'on the bit', so you should constantly be aware of the necessity of keeping the horse moving forward with the hindquarters engaged. Obviously, you must also be able to ask for, and keep, a correct bend to either direction.

A serpentine gives the opportunity to practise changing the bend so that the horse becomes more flexible. Only a gradual changeover is desired, with the horse being allowed plenty of time to alter through his length. The amount of bend, or change of bend, should match the curve you are trying to take. You will find in this exercise that your inside leg will be crucial for holding the bend and helping balance. Also, when you change bend remember that the control of the gait should be in your outside hand and this must be transferred at each changeover. As always, good co-ordination of aids is the best help.

IN CANTER

Do not attempt canter serpentines until the horse has learned collection, or his balance will easily be lost and he may change legs or become disunited. You also need to learn how to ride counter-canter and, later on, how to do a single flying change.

As you ride the movement, try to feel where the weight is. The horse may try to take more on his outside shoulder (opposite the leading leg) and, if he is allowed to do so, balance will be lost and eventually he may break gait, or change leg.

Once you reach the stage of including flying changes in serpentines, you are bound to get some anticipation. Any slight change in your weight or aids could seem like an indication to the horse that you are asking him to change. Great sensitivity is needed, together with positive aids that cannot be mistaken.

When riding flying changes do not have excessive bend at the moment of the changeover, it makes it far too difficult for the horse. If the hindquarters do not come round your inside leg when the aid is given the horse is more likely to change 'late behind'. This change of bend is critical to the smoothness of this movement. Beware of allowing the hindquarters to come 'in' in canter as this also makes it very difficult to achieve a correct change. Shoulder-in position throughout the movement will eliminate such problems.

Some of the serpentines require loops from true canter to true canter, in which case the usual preparation for a single change is required. Since, in this instance, it is to be performed from a curve rather than a straight line, the horse may find the positioning confusing. Try to ensure that, after you have come round the turn and are approaching the centre line, the horse is evenly balanced, and is accepting the aids properly. If any resistance occurs that cannot be rectified easily, ride forwards and do not attempt the change that time.

Some serpentines are ridden totally in counter-canter, in which case the bend should always be kept to the leading leg. When you are starting, you may have the horse's forehand nearly straight until such time as you both get the idea of changing direction but, as soon as possible, a correct bend should be kept.

Later on in the training, you will have to ride the counter-canter changes. As always, the basic principles regarding the gait, balance, collection and so on apply. Additionally, you should be extra careful with the positioning of the horse for the changes, so as to help him as much as you can in what can be a very awkward movement for him.

GIVE AND RE-TAKE
THE REIN

The Judge

The FEI definition states that:

> This requires the rider to push both hands forward to release the contact and then re-take it. This should be one continuous movement.

This exercise is not used very often in competition, but is a very useful test of the horse and rider's ability to maintain balance.

The rider should be expected to release the contact gradually for a few strides and then, equally carefully, re-take it. This can be done with a stretching of the arms and does not mean that the body needs to incline forward. However, this would not be particularly frowned upon unless there was excessive movement, or weight was put over the horse's forehand.

The horse is required to reach slightly forward towards the bit but, in every other respect, to stay in the same outline. There are various faults resulting from inadequate training for this exercise. You are required to know what they are, and the cause, so that you know how to penalise them. Key errors are:

1) Crookedness or deviation from the line, proving that the horse's straightness has not really been established and is over-reliant on the rider's aids. In addition, you should note whether the rider has tried to keep the horse straight with his legs, or whether control has been inadequate. This latter point may be noted in the rider mark at the end.

2) Alteration in the balance – falling onto the forehand as the rein is given. Generally this would result from a lack of established balance, loss of engagement, inadequate acceptance of aids, hollowing of the back or lack of impulsion.

3) Increase in speed. This often happens when the rein is given, but should be frowned upon, as any change in tempo or rhythm may cause irregular steps or imbalance.

4) Break in gait. Mostly, this occurs from lack of impulsion or engagement, but it can also arise from the rider having given the horse too much support from the rein which, when given away, allows the horse to 'fall apart'.

5) Resistance. If the horse shows resistance to the aids, especially as the reins are re-taken, this means that he was insufficiently prepared, both in his training and probably, for that moment, by the rider.

6) In canter, additional to the above, there is the correct sequence of steps to look for. Also, when assessing straightness, shoulder-in 'position' should be allowed for. You will also have to take into account the line on which the exercise is to be performed. This may be a diagonal, a long side of the arena, or on a circle. In each case the horse should remain on the prescribed line.

Sometimes during a test you will see an experienced rider give and re-take with an inside rein. Although not part of the test this should not be marked down unless, in your opinion, it is done to excess. In such a case a comment could be made in the rider mark. You should be aware of the use of this giving and re-taking which is of invaluable help to the rider as a test of the horse's self-carriage and, as such, may be a guide to you also. When a half-halt is employed to improve balance either just prior to, or following, a giving and re-taking of the rein, judgement should be made as to whether it improves the quality of the canter, in which case it would be perfectly acceptable, or whether it was used as a rather desperate measure to control something which was going wrong. Where giving and re-taking of the rein is specified the rider is only required to show this once for a stride or two not several times as some do. This is a misconception of the requirement on the rider's part.

GIVE AND RE-TAKE
THE REIN

The Trainer

While you will need to be aware of the requirements for competition (see FEI definition, page 147), you will be more concerned with the use of this exercise in everyday training, where it can be employed usefully at non-specific moments to test the horse's reaction, and to aid self-carriage. In tests, the rider is asked to perform this exercise with both reins but, during daily work, one or both reins may be given. For instance, on a circle, giving the inside rein only is a very useful way to discover whether the rider has the control sufficiently in the outside rein. It also makes the horse carry himself without leaning on the rein. Once the horse learns not to rely on the rider's hand, lightness and freedom of the shoulder can follow.

The outside rein may also be given, briefly, to find out how reliant the horse is on it, but also to encourage stretching of the muscles in the neck on that side. This is all helps to improve suppleness.

The pupil will soon discover how important it is to have the horse's hindquarters well engaged, together with good acceptance of the aids, in order to perform this exercise well. Correctness of gaits, straightness, regularity, rhythm and suppleness are all parts of the whole, and should be constantly checked.

At all times it will be necessary to check the rider's position to ensure balance is maintained. Any leaning forwards or alteration of weight should be prevented. Also make certain that the rein is not 'thrown' away and that it is picked up again gradually.

GIVE AND RE-TAKE
THE REIN

The Rider

The object of this exercise is to test whether the horse is in self-carriage, but very often it can be just as important to test yourself, to see that you are not in any way using the reins for support. Although you may tell yourself that you are not relying on the reins overmuch, it is not until the contact is broken that you discover the truth! There are two most important points to get right before this exercise can be of value. The first is to have a really good, secure position in the saddle; the second is to be able to feel and maintain a contact with the horse's mouth which does not interfere with his going forward or maintaining a steady head carriage. Only when you have mastered these points will you really be in a position to try this exercise.

When you do try it, be exceedingly careful how you do it. If the horse suddenly loses the security of your contact he may be taken by surprise, throw his head up, fall out of balance, break gait and so on. Similarly, when you take back the contact, if it is taken too sharply, the same kind of thing can happen. Clearly, this points to a gradual movement of your hands towards the horse's mouth to allow the contact to be broken and a similar gradual taking up of the feeling on the horse's mouth during the 're-take'. The contact should only be broken once, and only for a few strides, not, as I have seen some riders doing, trying to 'give' two or three times across a diagonal!

You may feel the horse stretch his neck and 'reach' for the bit or he may stay in the shape he is in already. Either way,

150

what you *do not want* to feel is any weight falling onto his shoulders or any alteration in the stride. Other common faults are:

Snatching : 'above the bit'. As you 'give' the rein, the horse should not snatch at your hands, trying to take more than you want to give – although this could be a signal to you that you may have been 'holding him together', rather than maintaining a sympathetic contact. If he puts his head up on the release of the rein you should be alerted to what may be a serious fault. Whenever the horse tries to get his head in the air, come 'above the bit', or hollow his back, it does mean a failure on your part, in that you have not taught correct engagement or acceptance of the bit. Without these two major points being correct, the horse will not be able to do his work as required.

Breaks in gait. If the horse breaks gait during the exercise, he is very probably not sufficiently 'on the aids', but mainly he is not yet in the balance needed.

Resistance. Very often, as the contact is re-taken, the horse will resist in some way. He may fight the bit by opening his mouth, crossing his jaw or tilting his head; he may simply break gait to a lower one; or he may swing his hindquarters, change direction and so on. You must be ready for any of these occurrences so that you prevent them, rather than having to correct. Good preparation is essential to all exercises.

Points to bear in mind during this exercise are:

1) Straightness. During the 'giving' of the rein in trot, the horse will be expected to stay straight, so you must use your aids evenly to encourage this. In canter, you may need to use shoulder-in position (see page 205) to prevent incipient crooked-ness. Your legs should be kept in the canter aid position and your seat should remain steady, as any change of weight may affect the horse's balance. As you pick up the contact, you

must take the bend to the leading leg or the horse may mistake what you are asking and come back to trot.

2) Rhythm. Whatever gait you are in, it is important that you ensure that the horse holds his rhythm before, during and after the giving and re-taking.

Finally, when you are learning yourself, or teaching the horse, it may well be easier to do this exercise on a circle to begin with, as it is often easier to achieve the necessary balance with the horse bent, rather than straight.

It is important to ensure the horse holds his rhythm.

CENTRE LINES

The Judge

ENTRIES IN TROT

It is always good to see an impressive entry, with rider and horse looking business-like and ready for action.

Theoretically, you should mainly observe the straightness, and any crookedness or wandering should be marked down. However, you should also certainly be aware of any lack of impulsion or engagement. If the horse's steps lack height or purpose, this will show up in the entry. If the horse is on his forehand you may almost see the withers as he comes towards you, and if he is overbending you will be able to see at least three plaits!

The transitions to and from halt will also tell you a lot about the engagement and submission. Up to Novice Level, of course, these transitions may be progressive, whereas by Elementary Level they should be almost direct. Personally, I would not be too strict about this until Medium Level, as I would prefer to see fluency rather than resistance – which may occur if the rider tries too hard.

If, for whatever reason, a crooked halt occurs it should be acceptable to you that a correction is made by taking the horse forwards to straighten him before the salute. Naturally, this could not earn such a high mark as a horse who halts straight in the first place.

From Medium Level upwards, you should begin to be strict about the transitions being direct, noticing any intermediate steps, which should be penalised.

ENTRIES IN CANTER

In the entry, the rider may need to employ some shoulder-in 'position'. This should not be excessive and should be removed as the horse comes into halt.

As with the trot, all transitions should be smooth, with no resistance. It is a primary concern that the horse remains engaged as, if he does not, all his weight will fall onto his shoulders and his rider's hands. If this happens, the hindquarters will not be in a position to move off correctly.

All work on the centre line should show straightness, balance, a steady, correct outline, rhythmic steps and a flexion to the direction of any oncoming turn or circle.

Trot on the centre line — Jane Bredin on Goya

CENTRE LINES

The Trainer

Straightness is one of the basic essentials in training; the hind feet following in the tracks of the forefeet. Horses, like people, are often 'one-sided', being more dexterous one way than the other. This can make them crooked, as it may be more comfortable for the horse to carry his hindquarters to one side or the other.

Getting horses to go forwards evenly from both leg aids is a major task, as is persuading them to accept an even rein contact. Until this is accomplished, centre lines can present big problems, especially in the transitions to and from halt. The horse who habitually tries to carry his quarters to one side will almost certainly accentuate this fault as he 'puts on the brakes'. In the move-off also, he will try to adopt what is, to him, a comfortable stance – which may mean dropping onto one shoulder or even evading the correct use of his hind legs by taking up his own bend. Any corrections which need to be made should be done with the help of shoulder-in. If, for example, the horse puts his quarters to the right in an entry, a right shoulder-in position should be taken. This can be held slightly (in training, even in halt if necessary) and again in the move-off, until the horse will accept straightening. Eventually it should also be possible to take a flexion either way in preparation for a turn or circle without the horse altering his footfalls.

During training, there will inevitably be anticipation of a particular movement while the horse is on the centre line, especially at halt. It is important, therefore, to ensure that horse and rider practise sufficiently to secure obedience.

155

CENTRE LINES

The Rider

Making sure that your entry to a test is impressive should be one of your priorities. Not only is it essential that your horse is able to go straight, but the very first movement you do should be good enough to make the judge sit up and take notice!

Getting past the A marker (if outdoors) can present a problem but, if you get as close as you can, you should be able to arrive on the centre line satisfactorily.

To keep the horse straight in trot you need to keep your eye on C, having the marker between the horse's ears. In canter, you may need some shoulder-in 'position' to prevent the hindquarters from swinging.

At the beginning of your training you should only ask the horse to come to halt through walk, paying particular attention to his acceptance of your legs and hands. Try to keep his hindquarters engaged in halt, ready for the move-off. This means that you should not allow him to come 'off the bit', nor should you take your legs away. Obviously, this maintenance of control should be done sympathetically because, if the horse feels trapped by the aids, he may panic. The move-off may be ridden progressively up to Novice Level but, as time goes on, both transitions must be direct.

The salute presents some problems unless you are careful because, if the horse feels any alteration in contact or weight, he may move, or attempt to do so. If you are ready for this and practise, the horse will become accustomed to this process.

When you have moved off you should straight away be preparing for your turn by carefully taking a flexion. This must only be an indication, so that the horse does not 'wobble'. Very often resistance to this request does cause trouble. Again, plenty of repetition will get you over the problem.

Very often riders say to me 'My horse accelerates on the centre line'. I think this is caused by a combination of trying too hard and being tense yourself, together with some antici-pation on the part of the horse. Obedience should be your keynote, together with plenty of experience to help conquer 'ring nerves'.

To keep the horse straight in trot, keep your eye on C.

TRANSITIONS AND HALTS

The Judge

The FEI definitions are:

The transitions

1) The changes of pace and speed should be clearly shown at the prescribed marker; they should be quickly made, yet must be smooth and not abrupt. The cadence of a pace should be maintained up to the moment when the pace is changed or the horse halts. The horse should remain light in hand, calm and maintain a correct position.

2) The same applies to transitions from one movement to another, for instance from the passage to the piaffe and vice-versa.

The halt

1) At the halt, the horse should stand attentive, motionless and straight, with the weight evenly distributed over all four legs, being by pairs abreast with each other. The neck should be raised, the poll high and the head slightly in front of the vertical. While remaining 'on the bit' and maintaining a light and soft contact with the rider's hand, the horse may quietly champ the bit and should be ready to move off at the slightest indication of the rider.

2) The halt is obtained by the displacement of the horse's weight on the quarters by a properly increased action of the seat and legs of the rider, driving the horse towards a more and more restraining but allowing hand, causing an almost instantaneous but not abrupt halt at a previously fixed place.

Your knowledge of how transitions should be ridden will help you to determine the degree of correctness. You will be aware that, up to Novice Level, all transitions may be progressive. While the acceptable degree of progression is debatable, I believe that your common sense will guide you in deciding whether a transition took too long. Much will depend on the stage of each horse's training, the difficulty of the exercise and whether, if the transition had been performed more quickly, it would have been detrimental to the performance.

Common sense will tell you whether a transition took too long.

At each level of training, a slightly higher degree of response will be desired over a shorter distance, but at no time would it be right to make abrupt or rough transitions. You are looking for a fluency of movement derived from the ability to 'change gear' with ease. When transitions have to be more direct, you should reward those who do them with precision and without apparent effort.

The causes of poor transitions are: bad preparation; loss of engagement or impulsion; stiffness through the horse's back; lack of submission to the aids. Train yourself to be able to spot these defects so that, when making comments, you pinpoint the appropriate cause.

TRANSITIONS AND HALTS
The Trainer

For the FEI definitions, see page 158.

TRANSITIONS

Transitions are the most crucial factor in your pupils' ability to put their movements together fluently. No good transition is possible unless the horse will answer the leg aids and simultaneously submit to bit pressure.

A novice horse, while learning, will be required to show only progressive transitions so, if the test says 'trot to halt', he may go through walk, and so on. This moment of progression is in order to allow for the adjustment of balance and straightness. Without these two commodities, fluency will never be attained.

As time goes by, direct transitions are included in tests, demanding further engagement of the hindquarters and collection. The half-halt (see page 167) will be of invaluable assistance in preparing for a transition. One or more may be needed in the lead up to any change of gait.

Teaching the horse to go smoothly from one gait to another is a matter of time and attention to detail. The chief problem for pupils is the co-ordination of aids, so this will be an area where they may need most help.

HALTS

Halts are generally spoilt by loss of balance or crookedness. Without good engagement, the hocks may well end up behind the quarters, thus preventing the ability to move forwards easily out of halt. At all times, horses should be trained to accept control by legs and hands simultaneously, otherwise resistance will be inevitable.

As with transitions, riders must be trained to use their aids together effectively in order to arrive at a good halt. Furthermore, maintaining a halt requires that the rider asks the horse to remain 'on the aids', and he accepts this instruction with immobility. Only from careful riding into halts and sympathetic control will the horse understand what is wanted.

A very precise halt with good attention.

161

TRANSITIONS AND HALTS

The Rider

TRANSITIONS

During your riding life you will ride millions of transitions, but how many, I wonder, will you ride really correctly? We change gait so often without enough thought or preparation and perhaps wonder why what comes after is not as good as it could be. If it is to be balanced, each gait must originate from a smooth changeover and, as balance is the essence of all riding, this is most important.

The first thing to ensure is that the horse is as straight as you can make him. In walk and trot this means a strict observance of equality of aids; in canter, it may require the use of some shoulder-in 'position'. The second important point is to have the horse consistently between leg and hand and to make him obedient. Through all transitions, the horse must accept the bit willingly. If he does not, the gaits will never flow freely and the whole performance will have a ragged appearance. Your attention to the communication between your hands and the horse's mouth will have a big influence upon the result.

If you have achieved these things, then transitions can be made accurately at a marker exactly when required. If you aim at being in the next gait as your leg passes a marker, then common sense should tell you that, to obtain this smoothly, a gradual change from the existing gait is necessary.

Progressive Transitions

Up to Novice Level all transitions may be progressive (for example, where a test asks for trot to halt, you may trot, walk and halt), so there is plenty of time to do them. A balanced transition is the aim, so it is necessary to focus your attention on the engagement of the hindquarters as being crucial to success. If this is accomplished and maintained, the hind legs will be under the horse, able to support and lighten the forehand and thus prevent the horse from leaning on your hands.

Getting from one gait to another should certainly neither look nor be an effort. If you have done your preparation properly, you may expect the horse to answer your aids immediately. You will prefer to obtain this obedience from light aids, i.e. those which obtain the result with minimum, effective effort. Transitions are often spoilt by a delay from the horse in answering, or by untidy, unnecessary movement of a rider's legs.

When you are learning, you may find it a problem co-ordinating the aids well enough – it can be awkward keeping the horse 'on the bit' – but time will help you to discover how to maintain contact whilst allowing the horse forwards.

Keeping the horse going forwards is essential not only in upward transitions but also coming down, as any loss of impulsion and engagement will permit the weight to fall onto the forehand. Therefore, do remember to sit into the saddle and use your legs firmly. Be prepared for adjustment of the new gait if necessary, using half-halts (see page 169) to re-balance if required.

Direct Transitions

These are the transitions which miss the intermediate gait or gaits, for example trot-halt, walk-canter, canter-halt, etc. If you have been thorough in your teaching of progressive transitions, your horse will be prepared to begin the direct ones. By the time you do so, you should have acquired a degree of collection which will make the transitions possible. At first, it may seem a real trial trying to keep your horse sufficiently 'together', but as your co-ordination and his collection improve, your transitions will become more accurate. As with all transitions, this accuracy is important for gaining marks in tests, but do not sacrifice your training for a precision which you may not have at the time.

As your training progresses towards Grand Prix, all transitions will gradually become established. If your work has been thorough, the ultimate test of this will be the transitions passage-piaffe-passage, in which the height, size and regularity of steps is achieved by having perfect mastery of the half-halt.

HALTS

All the previous comments regarding transitions apply to moving into and out of halts, from whatever gait. At Novice Level you should take plenty of time to make a halt. If you rush it, the horse may become crooked, or resist. If you do not keep the hindquarters engaged, the horse may be unable to balance properly. In progressive transitions or when coming to a halt it is most important that you use your seat and legs to keep impulsion forwards to the hands. Any pulling back or fixing of the hands will only prevent the horse from halting correctly. In the halts themselves, the horse should be totally straight from nose to tail and foursquare, so the aids must be used evenly to achieve this. (When you come into halt from canter, any shoulder-in 'position' used should be held until the moment of 'touch down', at which point equal aids should be applied.)

Many problems occur with halts that could be avoided by using common sense and greater sensitivity. Horses naturally do not stand still much unless they are asleep! Being made to stand 'on the aids' gives them a feeling of restriction from which they wish to escape. Resistance to the hands by swinging the hindquarters provides the horse with a means of evasion. While needing to maintain a firm contact with legs and reins you must never panic your horse by being restrictive. Do not try to correct a halt by pushing it sideways towards the line and never alter the hindquarters. Corrections should be made by riding forwards in a shoulder-in position. If the horse will not stand, practise the halt only briefly and when he is calm ask for longer halts.

It is important not to allow the horse to halt in a hollow outline with his hind legs out behind him. This can be a strain on his back and will make the following movement difficult for him. Getting a square halt can be a problem. The first essential is to be straight. Once this point is established the horse may be asked to alter a leg that is out of position by being brought more onto the aids with the help of a schooling whip.

HALF-HALTS

The Judge

The FEI definition of the half-halt is:

> The half-halt is the hardly visible, almost simultaneous, co-ordinated action of the seat, the legs and the hand of the rider, with the object of increasing the attention and balance of the horse before the execution of several movements or transitions to lesser and higher paces. In shifting slightly more weight onto the horse's quarters, the engagement of the hind legs and the balance on the haunches are facilitated, for the benefit of the lightness of the forehand and the horse's balance as a whole.

In tests you will not specifically have to mark half-halts; only the result of them. However, as with most things, better judgement can be made if you have experienced the feel of a good half-halt yourself. You will know, from the look of what is happening, whether a horse has truly given the rider what he wants as he uses it for preparation or correction within a movement. You will be able to assess the obvious faults and whether there are hidden stiffnesses or resistances, which can be the result of poor or hurried training. These will show up particularly in transitions and all collected work.

Competitors may need to employ half-halts for making corrections during a test (indeed, you could expect to see an experienced rider use them at any time) and it should be remembered that a half-halt is not a separate item which can be divorced

165

from the whole — rather, its use is essential to the whole. Therefore, the correct use of half-halts to improve the quality of the work should be totally acceptable. However, if they are detrimental for any reason (such as being overdone or incorrectly ridden), this should be taken into account when giving marks.

This demonstrates collection resulting from correctly ridden half-halts, but the off-hind should be further under the body for good collection.

HALF-HALTS

The Trainer

If your pupils are to achieve a good standard of riding, they need to master this exercise from an early stage. Naturally, their understanding of it will depend upon your ability to explain it – perhaps to demonstrate on their own horses the result of using it.

I have found that novice riders simply do not appreciate the necessity for frequent use of the half-halt, and therefore do not employ it automatically, as an experienced rider would. I have found with many riders that the build up to a correct half-halt comes from focusing on the horse's balance, which is relatively easy to feel, whether right or wrong. This makes riders use 'bringing together' aids, without the complication of placing too much emphasis on the halt. During this work they will learn the use of leg and hand together, and how to overcome those resistances which the horse may show. At the same time the horse will benefit by learning (if he does not know already) how to accept being 'put together'. This work can be done in any gait for a few strides at a time. Most novice riders will either drop impulsion or drop the contact at first but, when they have learned to maintain both and can keep the horse in a balanced rhythm, they should be ready to go a stage further.

In my own experience I have found that horse and rider appear to benefit from working on a circle first, doing transitions, achieving these without resistance to the aids and then progressing to an 'almost' transition – which, in effect, is what you want. This way they keep the horse going and can keep a regular stride. The horse learns to become more engaged from the work he is doing and, as the hindquarters come more under the body, he begins to lift and lighten the forehand. As time goes by, impulsion can be increased and collection requested, so that the rider is then in a position to use a half-halt whenever he needs to, as preparation or for increasing collection.

During test riding, you will require pupils to use half-halts to a greater or lesser extent to aid the degree of accuracy needed. They may be used during a movement to improve or correct the gait, or for their many other purposes. Being momentary actions, they are perfectly acceptable by judges, who would rather see a correction made and be able to give a higher mark than see less interference but less quality.

As training progresses towards advanced work the degree of aid co-ordination must necessarily increase. While a novice rider may get away with lesser co-ordination, an advanced rider cannot. Unfortunately there are many riders who lack this skill and who are not naturally talented. If you have a pupil in this category everything will be more of a struggle and will test your determination and patience.

Improving the horse by riding it yourself will be one option as resistance resulting from the rider's unco-ordinated aids may destroy new work being attempted. Although most pupils prefer, and actually benefit from, doing the training themselves there are occasions when a more professional approach is needed. Once the horse has overcome his worries and dislike of being brought together by the half-halts, the owner may be put up to be given the 'feel'.

In my experience novice riders do not make use of the half-halt and are, apparently, oblivious of its value. You must make clear how beneficial half-halts are to control and how control is necessary for balance. Putting a pupil on a trained horse is one way to teach them the feel of riding half-halts and how they are used to achieve collection.

HALF-HALTS

The Rider

Without satisfactory half-halts you will not progress very far, so it is crucial to learn to ride them properly. You need to use them frequently for control, while the horse needs them to help his balance and to learn to 'come together' — essential for collection.

At first, the half-halt will be used in its simplest form, as a steadying aid. This, depending on the degree of impulsion, entails either driving legs or holding legs, while the hands, receiving the energy, reduce or re-balance it. To know whether such a half-halt is necessary you must feel whether your horse's steps are in a regular rhythm, whether he can maintain them, and where most of his weight is at the time. If it is predominantly on the shoulders, you should try to transfer it to a more equal distribution over all four legs. Steadying aids and half-halts are not used in an isolated manner, but may need to be applied in a related series in order to take effect.

When the horse has understood and accepted a firmer momentary combination of leg, seat and hand, he should be ready to go a stage further and allow himself to be 'brought together' more in readiness for collection. Instead of merely re-balancing the horse, you should now use the half-halt to further engage the hindquarters, restraining the steps briefly to encourage a slightly shorter but higher stride. You should feel, first, a forward reaction to the use of seat and leg which, if accepted submissively by the horse's mouth, will enable him to round his back, lower his hindquarters, lift his forehand and become collected.

Obtaining this submission will require knowledge and sympathy. You must know how firm to be with the contact, making sure that it is not 'dead,' but the result of a 'feel and ease' action, and be certain that the hands do not cause the opposite effect to that required because they have 'blocked' the impulsion. At first, it may be almost impossible to co-ordinate the use of the aids to influence the horse correctly, so you will probably encounter resistance for some time. If resistance is persistant do not become downhearted. The horse does not find these aids easy to accept and will look for ways not to do so. The sort of thing you may encounter is an active objection by the horse fighting against the hands or even kicking to the leg aids. This must be dealt with by checking the aids you are giving to make sure that they are being applied in the right way. The horse may also resist in a less obvious fashion, that of stiffening his back or setting his jaw. He should be 'loosened' by the use of alternate flexions or by being made to bend by use of lateral work, especially shoulder-in. This suppling will remove all the stiffness which is preventing the half-halt from working. If the horse answers the legs (maybe with the aid of the schooling whip), the key to the problem will be in the mouth. If you are firm but sympathetic with your hands, using an action which 'asks', is patient for an answer and does not prevent the horse from going forwards, you should gradually get what you want.

So often, the effect of the half-halt is lost by the rider in one of the following ways: 'giving away' the contact to go forward; hanging on to it rather than using the 'feel and ease' action; using the seat and legs too much, demanding impulsion the horse is not ready for; not using seat and legs enough. To get it right requires skill, tact and experience which, given time, you will achieve.

The development of a 'deep' seat is an important factor in riding a good half-halt. Work on the lunge without reins and stirrups (on a safe horse with a knowledgeable trainer) is useful and as the seat gains in strength and security so co-ordination improves. Some people are naturally well co-ordinated while others struggle. If you are one of the latter some practise on a trained horse may help you acquire the feel.

PART SIX
Collecting and Lengthening

Although the horse is showing collection, his neck is somewhat overshortened.

COLLECTION

The Judge

The FEI defines the collected gaits as follows:

Collected walk. The horse remaining 'on the bit' moves resolutely forward, with his neck raised and arched. The head approaches the vertical position, the light contact with the mouth being maintained. The hind legs are engaged with good hock action. The pace should remain marching and vigorous, the feet being placed in regular sequence. Each step covers less ground and is higher than at the medium walk, because all the joints bend more markedly, showing clear self-carriage. In order not to become hurried or irregular, the collected walk is shorter than the medium walk, although showing greater activity.

Collected trot. The horse, remaining 'on the bit' moves forward with his neck raised and arched. The hocks, being well engaged, maintain an energetic impulsion, thus enabling the shoulders to move with greater ease in any direction. The horse's steps are shorter than in the other trots, but he is lighter and more mobile.

Collected canter. The horse, remaining 'on the bit' moves forward with his neck raised and arched. The collected canter is marked by the lightness of the forehand and the engagement of the hindquarters: i.e. is characterised by supple, free and mobile shoulders and very active quarters. The horse's strides are shorter than at the other canters, but he is lighter and more mobile.

Collected trot — head too high, back too hollow
Jennie Loriston-Clarke on Dutch Gold

With these definitions there are several main points to watch out for, with common denominators in all gaits:

Insufficient collection. Riders fail to engage the hindquarters sufficiently, preventing the possibility of lightening the forehand. This lack of engagement may be the result of inadequate response to the rider's leg aids, inactivity of the hind legs, tension or hollowing of the back, or resistance in the mouth. Whenever there is a lack of engagement there is likely to be labouring, and limitation in the execution of movements.

Overshortening of the steps. Riders do not always understand that, although in all gaits the steps may become shorter, this is not the criterion – the 'shortening' or gathering together of the frame is. Thus, while shorter, elevated, impulsive steps are a *consequence* of collection, short, inactive steps do not *constitute* collection. In true collection, therefore, the horse, responding to firm use of the rider's seat and legs, allows himself to be united through a round, supple back, stepping into the rider's hands without resistance. If the rider tries to achieve this without enough activity or impulsion, he will find that he has nothing but short, shuffling steps, with no suspension. The suspension is an important quality of the work in general; without it the horse cannot cover ground. Also, in canter, lack of it can inhibit the flying changes. Over- (incorrect) collection in this way can also destroy the correct sequence of the gaits.

False collection. This is the kind of collection that is made more by the rider's hands than by the seat and legs. It results in 'shortening of the neck', or a 'drawing back' from the hands. Any 'reeling in' of the forehand causes hollowing or tension in the horse's back, which in turn makes engagement of the hindquarters far harder for the horse.

False collection may be also identified by a loss of true sequence in the gaits, e.g. pacing not walking. The rider has, instead of bringing the horse forwards to his hand aids, allowed him to sit behind the leg. The horse's back then stiffens with the subsequent loss of correct footfalls. Similarly in trot, any tension created by restriction instead of correct collection may cause uneven or irregular steps. In canter, the restriction is reflected by a four-beat stride instead of a three-beat stride. False collection should be marked severely as it destroys the gaits and prevents the horse from progressing further. Although blame will be placed on the rider, each collected movement will be affected in some way and will, therefore, lose marks.

COLLECTION

The Trainer

Achieving correct collection (as defined on p. 175) is crucial to success in dressage competitions. Collected work is so often badly ridden, the gaits being sometimes spoilt by hasty attempts, or by asking for it before the horse is sufficiently prepared.

Good preparation is the key to success, the gaits being properly established in balance, rhythm and straightness. In addition, an essential element is willing acceptance of the aids. This can take considerable time and must not be rushed. Mistakes made in these early stages will certainly be paid for later on.

Without the development of the half-halt, collection is impossible, so a thorough understanding and execution of this is vital.

The object of your training must not only be to give your pupils success in the arena, it must be to produce correct work. Gold medals cannot be won on a basis of hasty attempts or short cuts. At the highest levels of competition, collection plays a major role. Study of its use and effect, its purpose generally and its capacity to facilitate ease of movement is a crucial part of your work.

Some less experienced trainers do not always fully appreciate that good extension depends upon the engagement achieved from collection. Many fairly poor trot gaits have been improved out of recognition by getting the horse collected first. Of course, you will meet resistance and evasion of the collecting aids. Horses do not find this work easy and they may put up objec-

Some horses object to collection.

tions. You must discover your own way through these situations, as each horse may be different. Basically, time and gradual increase of pressure to work will bring about the right result.

In order to be able to influence the horse in the right way, your pupils should be encouraged to achieve a deep seat and independence of their hands.

COLLECTION

The Rider

Understanding the principles of this issue is of prime importance. Feeling it is yet another of your main concerns. In the first place, you should try to learn why collection is so important to the work and to see that, without it, the horse will be at a big disadvantage.

Watching and learning about collection is most necessary and will help you to also find out what is should feel like. If you watch Advanced dressage you can observe the lowering of the hindquarters that occurs with real engagement. The horse's hind legs come under his body so that they are in a position to lift and lighten the forehand. You can start teaching this at a novice stage – in fact, it is important that you do. From the start of his training the horse must learn to engage, and should not be allowed to put weight on his forehand. The process, however, is very gradual. At each stage of training, as one degree of engagement is established, the next can begin.

You must be very careful that you combine engagement with the correct outline and acceptance of the aids. If you make a mistake in this aspect you could hinder the following work irrevocably. Use of the half-halt is crucial to your accomplishment of collection, so the novice horse should learn to accept it, and the degree should be gradually increased as time goes by.

Your horse cannot collect unless he is supple. Transitions, circles, shoulder-in and many other movements will help with this.

If you allow resistance to creep in, it will cause you many problems. Obedience to the aids will be a crucial factor in whether you accomplish collection. Activity is one of your first concerns. If the horse is idle, you will never arrive at what you want. Once he is active, his increased energy will give momentum.

A collected horse should not feel 'held together' in a grip, but as if the forehand and hindquarters are connected by a strong piece of elastic. Also, the gaits should feel purposeful, full of impulsion, with the steps covering ground. They should feel springy and give a sensation of 'lift' — the moment of suspension in trot and canter should be clear.

Although, technically, the steps may be shorter and higher than a working trot, do beware of overdoing this point and restricting them. Many attempts at collection are spoilt by losing energy and height, ending up with flat, shuffling steps.

Another major fault is when the horse's forehand is 'shortened' by collecting hands which are not supported sufficiently with the seat and legs. Always start with the hindquarters, bringing the energy through to your hands.

Creating the right degree of impulsion is not always easy. Too little and you have nothing to collect, too much and the horse may find it difficult to balance. It is very important that throughout the process of collection the horse is in self-carriage. This should be constantly checked by giving and re-taking the reins. The impulsion needed is brought about by engaging the hindquarters via transitions which are used to help the horse to lower his hindquarters. Half-halts should be employed to aid this process.

Well co-ordinated aids are essential and it is also important not to demand too much collection at one time but to build up gradually. A few steps may be asked for followed by actively riding forwards. In this way any restriction is limited and energy lost is quickly regained.

Any resistances should be dealt with sympathetically but firmly. Corrections should be made carefully, with much thought. Do not demand too much or go on for too long at a time. A tired horse cannot give of his best and collection can be a tiring business, especially in the learning stage. Finally, do remember that collection is not 'holding the horse together' but teaching him to 'carry himself' in a collected manner.

LENGTHENING THE TROT

The Judge

When judging this movement you should first determine whether the gait prior to the lengthening is correct. Then you will see the transition into the lengthening, which should maintain the qualities of rhythm and balance of the preceding steps.

At Novice Level the amount of lengthening cannot be specified (indeed, it is the quality rather than number of steps that counts), but you should see a clear difference in the stride. Do not be taken in by exaggerated steps, or extension, unless they are natural and you can see that there is more to come at a later stage.

The activity of the hind legs is all-important, and should show good flexion of the joints, with the legs working well underneath the hindquarters. Horses who 'thrust off' with the hind legs behind the quarters, or who go 'wide behind' should be penalised.

Hollowness of outline should also be dealt with severely as, without a rounded outline, good extensions will not be possible later on. Crookedness or irregularities in the stride are both bad faults but loss of rhythm, if momentary, is not a crucial issue (although it would not gain a good mark). Balance is very important and any loss will affect the steps seriously.

The transition returning from lengthening to the working gait is to be evaluated in the movement, and should show a resistant-free return to a correct gait with the outline, rhythm and balance being maintained.

180

LENGTHENING THE TROT

The Trainer

This could be one of your most testing tasks as, although there are many horses who do lengthen naturally and easily, there are equally many who do not. If you have chosen the horse yourself, you will have made certain that there is a natural flair. Even having done this, some horses temporarily lose the ability under the rider. However, this should be recoverable in time, as the horse learns to be balanced, engaged and collected.

Some horses do have to be coerced into making the effort with a good deal of help from the schooling whip, until they learn to respond properly to the aids. Others may only have the capacity to give one variety of lengthening (their maximum stride) and can never be improved, however hard you try. In such cases, clearly, the horse's ascent in pure dressage competition is limited. Horses with extravagant action, on the other hand, may need restraint from producing a really big stride before they have the balance, or until they can be sufficiently controlled.

The transitions into and out of the lengthened gait are of great importance in the building towards medium and extended movements. The rhythm, regularity, balance, straightness, outline and acceptance of the aids all have to be constantly checked. It may be advisable to teach pupils to rise to the trot until the horse is able to take their weight without hollowing, and until they are capable of sitting firmly, with independent hands. It can be distressing to see riders using the reins for support, or upsetting the gait through their insecurity in the saddle.

181

LENGTHENING THE TROT

The Rider

In tests which specify 'lengthening', you do not need to show extension but you do need to show a clear difference from the working gait. To achieve lengthened trot you first need a good, active working trot. This should be balanced, so that the horse can use his hind legs under his body to support his forehand. He should understand your aids well so that he will respond to a little extra use of your legs and go forward more. At the same time, he should allow himself to be controlled without resisting your hands, remaining in a rounded outline. If you rise to the trot to begin with you will be encouraging him to round his back, which will help him to develop the stride later on.

When you teach the horse lengthening, he may find it easiest on the long side of the school, being asked for only a few strides and then only if he is straight.

Try to concentrate on the transition at the beginning, making it smooth and getting gradually to the stride you want. If your horse is reluctant, use your schooling whip to assist your legs, but try not to let him hurry as a result. The rhythm of the working trot and the lengthening should be the same. If, on the other hand, your horse tries to dash off, restrain him carefully and only allow what you want. At the end, do not let the movement 'die out', but encourage the horse to gather himself together, engaging his hindquarters more under him. This, again, should be done gradually. You will need to use your legs firmly, and reduce the size of the steps carefully.

When your horse has learnt what is required on the long side of the school, progress to a diagonal. This is a little more difficult because of the angle of the turn onto it. Wait until he is straight before you ask, make sure that you look ahead, and ensure that you have ridden your return transition before you arrive back on the outside track.

The horse seems to be lengthening quite well but he has dropped onto his forehand and the rider is looking down.

LENGTHENING THE CANTER

The Judge

Any satisfactory lengthening of the stride in canter will be dependent upon the correctness of the preceding canter. The size and number of the strides cannot be specified but there should be a clear distinction between the working gait and the lengthening. Therefore, although the transitions may be gradual, they should also be definite.

The lengthening should be evaluated on the ability of the horse to remain in balance, maintain engagement, roundness and rhythm, be straight and submit to the rider's aids. He should cover ground in the moment of suspension. Any crookedness, weight on the forehand or speeding up of the rhythm is incorrect, as is any resistance or evasion in the return.

Any shoulder-in 'position' necessary to aid straightness and control should not be discouraged, so long as it is not excessive.

As with all judging there is necessarily considerable variety, from the limited to the scopey stride. It is never easy to assess the more limited horse as it does not coincide with the picture in your mind. Being fair is often hard as the inclination is to give only moderate marks. It is important to decide whether the natural canter is satisfactory and whether the rider has brought it along correctly in training. If the decision is in favour of the training then a good mark could be given for the lengthening if all the other requirements are present. A clever rider can make lengthening appear more than it is by riding clearly defined transitions thereby covering up a deficiency. Be aware of this possibility and be able to see what is happening.

LENGTHENING THE CANTER

The Trainer

Horses of different types lengthen in a variety of ways. Those with a good moment of suspension will cover ground while 'in the air'. Others will try to 'flatten' and gallop off, even altering the correct sequence of steps. This should, of course, be prevented and a strict tempo and rhythm adhered to.

Engagement is the key to good lengthening in canter. If it can be taken and held it will sustain the balance and make the return transition far more effective. Good co-ordination of the aids and an understanding of the half-halt will be most helpful in this respect, and will assist riders in avoiding the common error of relying too much on the reins in this exercise, failing to use their legs effectively to keep the horse engaged. This is particularly so in the 'return', when firm use of seat and legs is required.

You may have to vary the amount of lengthening in tests according to your pupil's level of riding and the horse's training. Also, if the test is on poor footing a reduced amount of impulsion may be necessary to avoid slipping and loss of confidence. While marks may be lost if the difference from the working gait is not obvious, teaching good transitions will help in this respect.

Shoulder-in 'position' will be invaluable in avoiding crookedness, and pupils should be encouraged to make use of it.

LENGTHENING THE CANTER

The Rider

Before you attempt any lengthening in canter you should first be able to sustain a good working canter. It is important that the horse is in self-carriage, well engaged and straight. If you have to use any shoulder-in 'positioning' this should be just sufficient to prevent the hindquarters from coming in. If you overdo it, the horse will find it all too difficult, so you are making a rod for your own back.

Correct engagement will produce a feeling of power from the hindquarters, and a sensation of the forehand being lifted. The horse's back should feel soft to sit on – not tense or hard. He should be accepting the bit, with his poll being the highest point of his neck.

Between each of the canter strides there should be a moment of suspension, during which the horse should 'cover ground'. Try to encourage this by asking for as much impulsion as you can without making the horse struggle.

It is important that you maintain your canter aids and sit firmly in the saddle. Do not lean forwards to let the horse hump his back.

When you ask for the lengthening, it should begin from the hindquarters. If you ease the reins too much the weight may tip onto the forehand, or the horse may take the opportunity to come 'off the aids'.

Remember that you do not have to shoot off into lengthened strides; you can build up the strides gradually, show a few that are your maximum at that level of training, and then reduce again carefully. So long as the difference between the working and lengthened gait is obvious, the transitions may be gradual. Later on in training, you will be able to attain the lengthened strides more quickly.

If you are showing lengthened strides on a diagonal, do allow for getting straight following the turn. Similarly, the return to the working gait must be achieved before you meet the track.

On a long side of the arena the horse may be tempted to put his quarters away from the wall. Watch out for this and be self-disciplined about constant correction.

You do not have to shoot off into lengthened strides.

MEDIUM AND EXTENDED TROT AND CANTER

The Judge

In all medium and extended movements the engagement is paramount. Failure in this area will cause loss of balance (horses going 'wide behind' or on the forehand), rhythm or irregularity.

Extended canter — Emile Faurie on Virtu

It will also impede the capacity to 'cover ground', and may cause loss of suspension. Similarly, any related drop in impulsion will result in inability to sustain the steps over the required distance. It will also affect all related transitions, preventing fluency and upsetting the subsequent movement.

A good dressage horse should be able to show a clear difference between his medium and extended movements and this ability should be valued highly. There are many who do not do this adequately because of limitation of stride. You should be clear about what you want to see and prepared to reward real difference. Be particular about any alteration of correct sequence (such as galloping off in extended canter) and also about any change of tempo in trot work and transitions.

Many horses become crooked, or hollow their backs when asked to go more forwards – they should not get good marks.

Extended trot – Emile Faurie on Virtu

MEDIUM AND EXTENDED TROT AND CANTER

The Trainer

Without good engagement and impulsion, extensions will never be produced. These two components should be strictly controlled throughout the training, being brought along steadily by degrees so that, from a build up of collection and energy, the horse is able to produce a maximum stride. The medium gaits are a lesser expression of the lengthening, regulated through obedience and control to show a distinct difference.

If the horse is trained properly he should be able to lengthen his stride without loss of balance or engagement, and keep an exact rhythm. If the correct criteria are applied through transitions as well as when lengthening, good cadence should ensue, with clear moments of suspension. This precision of stride, coupled to his own control, should allow the rider to start, sustain and finish movements with clarity.

Good extensions involve much activity and movement under the rider, and can sometimes be difficult to sit on. Work without stirrups at all stages will provide greater depth of seat, making it possible for the pupil to absorb the movement.

Suppleness in both parties is essential to success. It provides the horse with more flexibility, enabling greater freedom and making him more comfortable to ride.

Many horses have a limited ability to show sufficient difference so you may be unable to produce what you really want, the medium gait being the maximum possible. This problem should be explained to pupils so that they are not disappointed by a lesser mark for the extensions. Both the trainer and pupil must then do their best.

MEDIUM AND EXTENDED TROT AND CANTER

The Rider

You will have already introduced your horse to basic lengthening, which he should be able to perform willingly, in a balanced, rhythmic and obedient manner, remaining straight and showing a clear difference, with definite transitions.

The development towards the bigger variations is evolved from greater activity and engagement, controlled by the use of half-halts and suppling exercises to provide collection.

Once this has been achieved medium work can take place, making sure that all the fundamental issues are constantly checked. Only by taking all the ingredients on to a higher degree can extension then follow.

A true dressage horse should have the ability to produce a difference between his medium and extended work and this should become possible from a systematic process of training. There are a few, however, who are not so well blessed and are restricted in action by their conformation. Such a horse will never become one of the 'greats' but, with careful training, can sometimes surprise.

Your own security in the saddle will greatly affect the ability of your horse to produce extension – you can only acquire the necessary control over impulsion if you are able to sit firm. Your seat must be independent of your hands and you must be as supple as possible to absorb the movement – which can be very unseating sometimes.

The types of problem you may encounter arise from those horses who do not wish to respond sufficiently, or those who

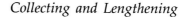

Some types need rousing . . .

try to take charge. The former will need some rousing by being made more obedient to the driving aids and may need some coercion into making the effort. The other type need restraint, but this should be done carefully so as not to destroy their inclination for forward movement, but merely temper it down. If overexuberance is allowed to continue many problems can arise.

There are many types of lengthening of steps. In trot, a good feeling is one of lift, cadenced spring and ground covered, with the horse's back soft and easy to sit into. A bad feeling is if it seems flat, joggling, or fast and leaning on your hands. In canter, a good stride should feel like a controlled uphill 'bound' with roundness and lift, its rhythm remaining entirely steady. Poor strides are manifested in quickening, pulling forward or hollowing of outline, the weight tipping you 'downhill'. If you recognise any of these descriptions it may give a clue as to whether you are on the right track. If not, return to base!

PART SEVEN
Lateral Movements

The object is to see whether the horse will move away from the rider's leg.

LEG-YIELDING

The Judge

The FEI definition states:

> The horse is straight, except for a slight bend at the poll, so that the rider is just able to see the eyebrow and nostril on the inside. The inside legs pass and cross in front of the outside legs. The horse is looking away from the direction in which he is moving.
>
> Leg-yielding is the most basic of all lateral movements and should be included in the training of the horse before he is ready for collected work. Later on, together with the more advanced movement shoulder-in, it is the best means of making a horse supple, loose and unconstrained, for the benefit of the freedom, elasticity and regularity of his paces and the harmony, lightness and ease of his movements.

Although leg-yielding does not appear in any current tests, it has very occasionally been asked for in competition, the object being to see whether the horse will yield and move away from the rider's inside leg. This should be done strictly in control, the horse being straight except for a slight flexion at the poll. The horse should not 'run' sideways but should advance equally, forwards and sideways. The steps should be of equal size, neither too wide nor too shallow. They should show a moment of suspension between each pair of diagonal legs and should be regular and in a clear rhythm.

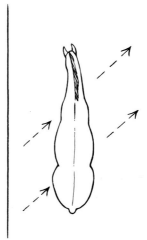

Leg-yielding

As a judge you should be aware of the value of leg-yielding, not as a movement in the test, but as a training exercise at home. Its introduction to the horse in his early training is essential to obtaining a satisfactory response to the rider's inside leg aid. The horse should instantly respond to pressure by either yielding more to the bend, or by stepping forwards and sideways. The rider must acquire the ability to use the inside leg for this purpose. The exercise may be ridden at all gaits but to a lesser degree in canter.

Although leg-yielding is primarily used as a training aid it may well be incorporated by the rider into the work while a test is taking place. If concerned that the horse has an unsatisfactory bend, the rider may well leg yield for a stride or two. It may also be used to recover from a situation where something has gone wrong, such as deviation from a line. In this circumstance the good judge will accept the rider's momentary correction as a necessity to improve the quality of the work. As this is the chief aim of riding dressage the rider should not be penalised.

LEG-YIELDING

The Trainer

For the FEI definition, see page 195. Leg-yielding is the initial introduction to lateral work and an important exercise by which a rider can gain more attention to his inside leg. It is used to teach a young or novice horse to move away from the rider's inside leg. In practical situations, leg-yielding can be used to obtain more bend and thus supple the horse; to move him in or out on a circle as a way of improving control and balance, and to teach him more about the aids. Riders should therefore incorporate it into the training, not so much as a complete movement, but more as a means of brief correction.

You, as trainer, should be quick to spot horses who 'cheat' or evade by taking small steps so that they do not have to use themselves. Riders, also, may need correction if they fail to keep the hindquarters behind the forehand, allowing the horse merely to bend his neck and lead with his outside shoulder. Too many riders draw the inside leg back to give the aid. This is incorrect as it invites the hindquarters to move away but does not achieve any flexion beneath the rider.

LEG-YIELDING

The Rider

The FEI definition of this exercise can be found on page 000. The aids for leg-yielding are as follows:

The inside leg applied on the girth.

The outside leg behind the girth.

The inside rein asks for a very small flexion.

The outside rein controls the speed and gait.

The horse should be straight through his body, giving just a slight flexion to your inside hand. Although he moves away from your inside leg, you should not draw that leg back, but keep it on the girth. If you have difficulty making the horse move over, use your schooling whip to help you. Control the impulsion with both legs but with the inside one predominant; your outside leg should prevent the horse from rushing sideways.

When starting the exercise, ask for only a few steps sideways, then a few forwards and so on, until the horse understands and you have discovered how to co-ordinate your aids.

When learning to leg-yield, most horses try to take the forehand over leaving the hindquarters trailing. It is vital that the horse does not cheat in this way as the whole point is to get even sideways movement from the whole horse. You must make sure that you pay attention to this fact and learn to feel what the hindquarters are doing.

SHOULDER-IN

The Judge

The FEI definition is as follows:

> The horse is slightly bend round the inside leg of the rider. The horse's inside foreleg passes and crosses in front of the outside leg; the inside leg is placed in front of the outside leg. The horse is looking away from the direction in which he is moving.
>
> Shoulder-in, if performed in the right way, with the horse slightly bent round the inside leg of the rider, and at the correct angle, is not only a suppling movement but also a collecting movement, because the horse at every step must move his inside hind leg underneath his body and place it in front of the outside, which he is unable to do without lowering his inside hip. Shoulder-in is performed 'along the wall' at an angle of about 30 degrees to the direction in which the horse is moving.

In tests, shoulder-in is ridden in various positions in the arena; on the centre line, on the long side coming towards C, or on the long side towards A. If you are positioned at C, the easiest place to see the angle is on the centre line, the next on the side towards C, and the most difficult on the side towards A. There can be an optical illusion about the latter which, seen from behind from C, often appears to have little or no angle. Seen from the position of H or M the same movement may appear perfectly satisfactory. Varying angles can be seen clearly enough, particularly if the eye focuses upon the inside hind leg and outside foreleg. In a good shoulder-in the alignment of this diagonal pair will be predominant and, if maintained, will normally indicate that adequate balance, bend, collection and impulsion are present.

Faulting the various discrepancies is what you are trained (or training) for, but these assessments are never easy. I think it would be fair to say that a mark of four (insufficient) could be given for the following: bend only in the neck; a good deal of resistance; irregular or very uneven steps.

A good shoulder-in will show well maintained collection, sustained impulsion, good submission and a clearly marked stepping of the inside hind leg well under the horse's body.

The use of shoulder-in 'position' to gain control of the forehand, prepare the horse for various movements and prevent incipient crookedness is dealt with at appropriate points throughout the text. Used correctly, it is a valuable tool for the rider: it should not be penalised unless its use is excessive or incorrect.

Shoulder-in

SHOULDER-IN

The Trainer

In any exercise your job is to make it as easy for your pupil (horse or rider) as possible. If neither know the exercise, it may be simpler for you to ride the horse first to teach him, and then help the rider. Sometimes this is not possible but, even if it is, in my opinion much valuable experience is lost if the rider does not at some stage grapple with the problems himself. This may take longer but if you are a calm, confident teacher and can inspire patience in your pupils, they not only learn so much more but also acquire a great deal of satisfaction from the achievement.

If you are trying to teach the combination of horse and rider together, then explanation of the exercise is the first necessity. Every teacher has their own way of explaining what is expected of the horse and, so long as you are clear on the FEI definition, you can put it in your own words. First tell your pupil what the exercise is, and explain the aids:

Inside leg on the girth to maintain bend and impulsion.

Outside leg behind the girth to assist the inside leg in keeping the horse correctly bent and going forwards.

Inside rein directs the forehand in from the track and maintains flexion.

Outside rein keeps control over the gait and maintains the angle.

The next step is to decide how to arrive at the end result. Beginning from walk or even halt to show the rider the angle he has to take is often advantageous. You can actually stand the horse in the position you want, get the rider to look down to see the three tracks upon which you want the horse to travel, and explain exactly what you want done with each hand and leg.

Stand the horse in the position you want and get the rider to look down.

Following this, you may wish the horse to proceed in a slow walk using half-halts, or even walk a few steps, stop, and go on again so that the rider has time to think what he is doing and can correct anything that is going wrong. Most riders use far too much inside rein to try to bring the forehand off the track, which merely creates a bend in the neck, while the forelegs remain on the track. A better understanding and firmer use of the outside rein in conjunction with the inside leg will gradually give the rider some clarity of the feel of the exercise. Even at the early stage, the use of the outside leg should not be neglected. The rider should be made very aware of the need to obtain bend throughout the whole horse, not being allowed to put too much accent on the front end of the horse but being made to remember the 'engine' at all times.

A small degree of shoulder-in, and only a few steps at a time is acceptable to start with, the rider then being asked to circle or straighten according to your wishes.

Once the exercise has been understood by both parties, it may be developed over longer distances, and then in trot. Once this is achieved, it can be used for its real purposes, which are suppling the horse, increasing collection, giving the rider greater control over the forehand and 'positioning' the horse prior to various other exercises such as lateral work and, in its smallest degree, for all corners and circles. You should, indeed, help the rider to understand the value of thinking 'shoulder-in aids' much of the time, so that he can balance and place the horse's forehand, thus making all such work easier.

Later on, the concept of taking a shoulder-in 'position' will be invaluable to the pupil in correcting any incipient crooked-ness in canter, for correcting quarters-in and in preparation for lateral work, changes and so on.

When the time comes for the pupil to ride tests which include shoulder-in, a greater degree of accuracy is necessary. I strongly advise you to watch pupils from C position in the arena to see them as the judge will see them. Only then will you really know whether angles are satisfactory and maintained, and whether the movement is begun and finished neatly at the designated markers. Maintaining good collection, impulsion and submission through the exercise will be vital to its quality.

SHOULDER-IN

The Rider

Many riders find shoulder-in one of the hardest exercises to learn, but it is ultimately one of the most useful, giving a control over the forehand which facilitates preparation for all exercises. It may be helpful, at first, to ride a trained horse to discover how to use the aids and to feel the angle required. Later, however, you may wish to train your own horse, and this will open up a host of possible difficulties to be overcome.

First of all, it will be necessary to know how to use the aids to good effect. Also, you need to teach the horse in an arena with a wall or fence so that the angle (maximum 35 degrees) can be assessed. To obtain any angle you must be capable of flexing the horse to the inside and placing the horse's forelegs slightly in front of the track, whilst keeping the hindquarters on the track. The actual position you want is the inside foreleg in from the track, the outside foreleg and inside hind leg on the same track and the outside hind leg on a third track. Your legs will be keeping the horse going forwards while the inside rein directs the forehand off the track. In this moment your inside leg on the girth should ask the horse to bend and, at the same time, go along the fence or wall. Your outside rein receives this drive from your inside leg and assists the inside rein in controlling the angle. Your outside leg should be behind the girth to prevent the hindquarters from swinging outwards and also to ask for the bend round the inside leg.

Co-ordinating these aids can take some time to achieve. Loss of co-ordination results in several faults, the most common of

204

which are: curling the neck round with the forelegs still on the track; keeping an angle but pushing the hindquarters out; varying the angle; causing resistance; losing impulsion and creating more angle than the horse can correctly maintain (which may provoke the previous two faults). The horse may also have trouble in co-ordinating his limbs and thus frequently fall out of balance, so you should constantly help him by checking your own position and use of the aids, and by reacting sympathetically.

It will be very difficult to ride shoulder-in without some degree of collection, so you must be prepared to spend several weeks teaching the horse to 'come together' submissively by the use of half-halts. These will probably be taught in walk to start with, followed by trot so, if you follow this sequence, it may well be best to begin shoulder-in also in walk.

Attempting to find the right 'feel' can often be puzzling. In this exercise particularly, there is sometimes a conflict between what you think *feels* right and what your trainer or the judge tells you *is* right. This is because, in a correct shoulder-in on three tracks, the amount of angle does not always feel enough so, in order to make it seem better, you try to take more angle than is necessary. The main points to try to feel are: a bend throughout the horse; the horse's inside leg coming under your seat with a soft swinging movement of his back; the shoulders taking equal weight with the forehand up in front of you, and an even contact with the mouth. (Although it should be possible to give and re-take the inside rein and still ride the exercise. This action is the ultimate test to see whether you have the position and control correct. If the horse remains steady you can be pretty sure you have achieved what you want.)

SHOULDER-IN 'POSITION'

Once you are fully conversant with the aids for shoulder-in, you can begin to explore the value of shoulder-in 'position'. This can be described as the rider 'thinking' of shoulder-in, in circumstances where he does not want the full movement, but rather the associated control, especially over the horse's shoulders. Examples of this would be before turns, circles and

Training shoulder-in — Jennie Loriston-Clarke

corners, where the horse must not 'lie' on his inside shoulder, nor should his outside shoulder 'escape'.

A horse who has already been taught the shoulder-in exercise will allow you to 'position' him, by flexing his spine under the saddle (not through the neck), thereby keeping his forehand fairly straight, but with his forelegs fractionally and momentarily in from the track.

From this 'positioning', you gain control of the forehand and, by increased use of your inside leg, you bring the horse's inside hind leg further beneath his body, thereby facilitating better balance. The aim is to 'prepare' and 'position' concurrently. Your outside rein should be controlling the speed, and the position of the horse's outside shoulder. The inside rein is directive, bringing the inside foreleg into position but not allowing the horse to step to the inside. Your outside leg will control any outward swing of the hindquarters and will, in fact, bend the horse slightly round your inside leg – which will be keeping up the impulsion. Both legs act to keep the horse up into his bridle.

As soon as the movement being ridden is commenced, the actual 'positioning' may be ceased, but the associated control – especially that over the shoulders – should be retained.

Eventually, the horse will need to respond to changes of 'positioning' for changes of direction quite quickly, so it is important to build a sound basis from an early stage, constantly checking the balance which will enable the horse to answer the aids.

In time, you will find that taking a shoulder-in 'position' can be invaluable in correcting any incipient crookedness in canter, especially when the horse is tending to swing his quarters in.

Although 'positioning' is invaluable, it can be overdone which in itself causes problems, especially in canter. Whereas in trot the leg sequence allows the horse to move in shoulder-in with a good deal of bend, in canter it does not. Thus it is important that any 'positioning' is taken with care without excessive angle. This may be gauged by the feel of the horse's response in respect of any resistance. If the 'positioning' is too great the gait will labour causing possible 'breaks' or a changing of leg. This may well be associated with tension in the back, resistance in the mouth or anxiety. If any of these problems occur reduce the angle of the position at once and pursue it more gradually.

HALF-PASS, TRAVERS AND RENVERS

The Judge

The FEI definitions are:

Half-pass. This is a variation of travers, executed 'on the diagonal' instead of 'along the wall'. The horse slightly bent round the inside leg of the rider, should be as close as possible parallel to the long sides of the arena, although the forehand should be slightly in advance of the quarters. The outside legs pass and cross in front of the inside legs. The horse is looking in the direction in which he is moving. He should maintain the same cadence and balance throughout the whole movement.

In order to give more freedom and mobility to the shoulders, which adds to the ease and grace of the movement, it is of great importance, not only that the horse is correctly bent and thereby prevented from protruding his inside shoulder, but also to maintain the impulsion, especially the engagement of the inside hind leg.

Travers. The horse is slightly bent round the inside leg of the rider. The horse's outside legs pass and cross in front of the inside legs. The horse is looking in the direction in which he is moving.

Travers is performed 'along the wall' or, preferably, on the centre line, at an angle of about 30 degrees to the direction in which the horse is moving.

Renvers. This is the inverse movement in relation to travers, with the tail instead of the head to the wall. Otherwise the same principles and conditions are applicable as at the travers.

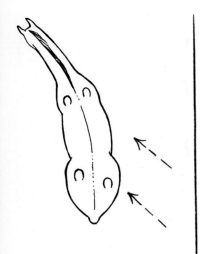

Half-pass

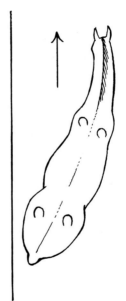

Renvers

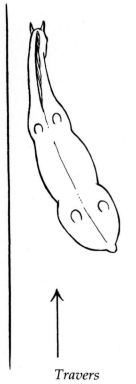

Travers

Half-pass left in trot, rider leaning wrong way – David Hunt on Fortuin

Half-pass left in trot (different angle) — Isabel Werth on Fabienne

211

Travers – Carl Hester on First Class

You will see many variations of this work. These can range from quarters leading to trailing, too much bend, almost no bend, incorrect bend, bend only in the horse's neck, insufficient collection or impulsion, loss of outline, varying angle, passage-like steps and the opposite – steps which drop height as the movement begins.

As with all judging your first priority is the gait, which should remain true – there should be no change in suspension, rhythm or balance. The trot gait can become too slow in tempo if the horse 'dwells' and does not go sufficiently forward. He can also try to become less engaged and to drop impulsion. If he manages to do this in canter, the gait will almost surely become four-beat. Loss of engagement can also allow tempo to *increase*: the horse may try to 'scrabble' across instead of retaining his balance and cadence. All the foregoing faults are serious, as any defect which affects the gaits or makes the horse struggle is bad training.

You will hope to see all lateral work ridden with a uniform curve through the horse's length, and you should be particular about correct angles. Any wavering, accentuated angles that make the horse flounder or impede forward movement are unsatisfactory. Too little angle is equally valueless.

At Medium Level, although accuracy is always important, I would rather see less precision but a good lateral movement, well maintained. I think this is important to the horse's future. If he is pliable enough he will be able to comply on both counts – which, of course, is the aim – but in training this is not always possible. The horse should be helped to feel comfortable with his work and everything made as simple as can be. I believe marks should reward riders who have this in mind, provided that there are no other particular faults. Later on, once the Advanced work is established, accuracy becomes a more important factor, and failure in this department should be penalised. This particularly applies in the zig-zags where exact numbers of steps or strides are specified. The rider must show the ability to judge and control the degrees of angle and distance as well as maintaining the quality of the gait, and riding the required steps or strides. In all lateral work the rider should sit with the horse, not lean away from the direction thus impeding the flow.

HALF-PASS, TRAVERS AND RENVERS

The Trainer

For FEI definitions, see page 208. It does seem that lateral work is a real bugbear for some people. The necessary co-ordination of aids eludes them, causing all manner of complications. The work can also be difficult for the horse, if insufficiently prepared. Thus you may have many details to iron out with both parties, and this can be a nuisance, hindering progress. It is important, therefore, to discover your pupil's limitations in these exercises. Do not allow pressure to be put on the horse until a clear understanding is achieved.

Prepare the combination by work on shoulder-in, incorporating the half-halt. This will give control of the gait and the forehand, and engage the inside hind leg. Also work the partnership on circles of approximately 10 m to achieve a uniform bend of the right degree.

Starting the work in walk will probably give most partnerships the best chance of getting together.

HALF-PASS

In half-pass, it will be necessary to make riders realise the importance of presenting the horse's forehand towards the marker at which he has to arrive. Many riders try to push the horse across sideways in an endeavour to keep him parallel to the side of the school. They should be riding towards the marker with a flexion to that direction, the remainder of the bend being achieved with their legs. This produces the half-pass which, as collection is increased, brings the horse parallel.

If the forehand precedes the hindquarters it is relatively simple, by greater use of the outside leg aid, to bring the quarters more round the inside leg, thus obtaining the required result. However, if the hindquarters lead, an inevitable loss of momentum and freedom occurs – with ensuing problems such as irregularity of rhythm and stride.

TRAVERS AND RENVERS

All the same criteria apply to travers and renvers. They are simply ridden on a long side or centre line instead of on a diagonal. There may be some adjustment for the rider to make mentally, as he prepares the horse for renvers in trot, in that he has to change the bend, but practice in walk first should iron out any confusion. Since renvers on the track in canter can only be ridden in counter-canter this does not arise, because the bend will remain to the leading leg.

The shoulder-in position will be invaluable at the beginning and end of all lateral exercises for the purpose of straightening.

Most riders seem to find it a hardship to use their inside leg sufficiently in lateral work. Without it, impulsion and bend cannot be maintained and the exercises will fail.

The rider's position must constantly be checked as any crookedness will prevent the aids from having the right influence, it will also be a hindrance to the horse in respect of balance. In all lateral work the rider's weight may be placed a little onto the inside seat bone to aid the flow and to give the inside leg maximum contact. The upper body should be aligned to the horse, that is to say, the rider's shoulders should be square to the horse. There should be no collapsing of the waist in either direction as this will diminish the influence of the seat. Also, the rider must keep the head upright and look towards the marker to which the horse is heading. Only by doing so will the correct angle and bend be kept.

Rein contact should be such that control of the gait, the collection etc. is maintained by the outside hand with the inside hand keeping a light control of the bend. Any restriction by the inside hand will prevent the horse from going forwards and this will cause loss of impulsion and resulting difficulty.

HALF-PASS, TRAVERS AND RENVERS

The Rider

Although many people tell me that their horse cannot go sideways, I have found that it is generally the rider who has not found the necessary co-ordination, and does not understand the correct position in which to place the horse!

There are three exercises that you should first establish clearly in your mind and be able to put into practice:

1) Be able to ride, and maintain a correct bend on, a 10 m circle.

2) Be able to ride half-halt.

3) Be able to ride a correct shoulder-in.

In performing these movements you should have discovered how to control the impulsion, how to use the leg aids to hold a bend and how to position the horse as a preparation.

TRAVERS

This movement may be the easiest to start with as you have the side of the arena to follow and the horse more readily puts his hindquarters in. You should probably start in walk until you can work in unison. Do not attempt many steps to start with and ensure that you make the horse straight immediately after any steps of lateral work.

216

HALF-PASS

Once you have mastered the basic idea of travers, you can attempt the half-pass on a diagonal line. Again, do not try for too many steps at first and make sure you do not allow any drop in impulsion. Your inside leg is responsible for maintaining this and, however contradictory you may find it, you must use this consistently to hold the bend and to keep the horse forward. Do not make the mistake of bending the horse's neck more than his body. He will find this restrictive, and be unable to go forward properly. In trot and canter you will need to obtain some collection as, without it, the horse cannot perform the exercise.

One fatal fault is to try to make the horse parallel to the side of the arena without first riding him towards the arrival marker. He should look at the marker and his shoulders should be positioned towards it. He can subsequently become parallel once he is sufficiently collected and bent round your inside leg.

If you find that you cannot get the movement right, always check on the position of the forehand first, then make sure the horse is answering your outside leg while sending him forward with your inside leg. Whatever you do, do not let the hind-quarters lead. This can only make it so awkward for the horse he will be bound to put up resistance.

RENVERS

In renvers, all the same principles apply but you can ride this on a long side or centre line. In trot an alteration of the bend is called for. As you come round the short end of the school, simply ride the forehand off the track and gradually alter the bend. It is not so difficult as it sounds, so long as you do not worry the horse by hustling him. In canter, (which will necessarily be counter-canter) the bend should remain to the leading leg.

In all the lateral work, co-ordination is hard until it becomes automatic. You may find it complicated but your horse will find it perfectly possible, if he is correctly bent and positioned.

A very nice picture with the horse accepting his rider's aids and moving freely in left half-pass.

218

PART EIGHT
Advanced Work

Horse and rider show good balance in this counter-canter.

COUNTER-CANTER

The Judge

The FEI definition is:

> This is a movement when the rider, for instance on a circle to the left, deliberately makes his horse canter with the right canter lead (with the right fore leading). The counter-canter is a suppling movement. The horse maintains his natural flexion at the poll to the outside of the circle, and the horse is bent to the side of the leading leg. His conformation does not permit his spine to be bent to the line of the circle. The rider, avoiding any contortion causing contraction and disorder, should especially endeavour to limit the deviation of the quarters to the outside of the circle, and restrict his demands according to the degree of suppleness of the horse.

In all the counter-canter work, balance and self-carriage are of prime importance. These qualities cannot be present unless the horse is well engaged, supple, submissive and collected. If any of these ingredients is lacking, there may be a loss of correct sequence of the steps, and labouring.

Whenever the gait is imperfect the penalty should be quite severe. Good collection is the key to this exercise, which means, of course, having sufficient impulsion to achieve and sustain it. At all levels, the degree of collection is relative to the difficulty of the movement.

One common fault is if the horse changes legs. Clearly, this is either a disobedience or the result of loss of balance. Some-

221

times the horse anticipates a change, or the rider may lose the bend. Whatever the reason, the movement is destroyed. If the horse continues on the wrong lead or is disunited he would deserve a very low mark indeed. In fact there may be occasions when 0 has to be given for the movement if the rider fails to get any true canter at all, but of course this must be clearly checked as often there may be some other factor involved such as a transition.

Most problems seen in counter-canter stem from the inability of the rider to ride in shoulder-in position in order to control the forehand. So often the weight is taken on the horse's outside shoulder which unbalances him and will enable him to change leg if he wishes.

Also frequently seen is the rider leaning away from the leading leg. This also unbalances the horse and prevents the rider from effectively using the inside leg. As this is vital to the energy of the gait and the bend, its position is crucial. Any weight taken on the outside seat bone may encourage the horse to change leg.

The rider should be asking for the bend by keeping the outside leg behind the girth which is additionally telling the horse which leg he is to remain on. If the outside leg aid is not used sufficiently, or not maintained, the movement may be lost.

As far as the rein aids are concerned, the rider should always have control of the gait and collection in the outside rein, with light assistance from the inside rein which is asking for the required flexion to the leading leg. Any bending of the neck of the horse rather than a uniform curve through his length will inhibit freedom and balance. The balance in this exercise is essential not only to its quality but also to the ability of rider and horse to do flying changes at a later date. Any lack of balance, therefore, should be marked down. It can also not be emphasised enough that without adequate collection the movement is impossible to ride and will look ungainly and ugly.

COUNTER-CANTER

The Trainer

For the FEI definition, see page 221

THE HORSE

The first essential is to have established a correct, true, collected canter in good balance.

To start with, a simple loop approximately 3 m in from the track should provide a sufficient test for the horse. On no account should there be any sudden alteration of direction; the whole movement should be ridden gradually. The horse must remain collected and be slightly flexed throughout to the leading leg. Beware of loss of engagement, weight falling away from the leading leg or too much bend in the neck.

As time goes on, the degree of collection is increased so that it is possible to ride the more difficult movements. However, be careful never to allow the horse to struggle in this exercise, as this would put undue strain on his back muscles.

THE RIDER

Any stiffness through the horse will be a handicap, so do make sure that the horse is supple enough before allowing pupils to attempt this exercise.

One of the hardest things for the rider, I have found, is maintaining control with the outside rein. There is a tendency to curl the neck inwards and be unable to give and re-take the inside rein. Only when the rider finds that he can support the horse from the use of leg aids and outside rein, and help him to find his own balance, will he be able to ride this movement effectively.

The rider may also find directing the horse difficult without taking the bend away from the leading leg. Initially, it will not matter if a small opposite flexion is taken to simplify a movement. As rider and horse get together you can first straighten, then produce the correct flexion.

Riders also tend to put too much weight on the outside, rather than the inside seatbone. This leaves them at a disadvantage, allowing loss of overall balance.

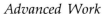
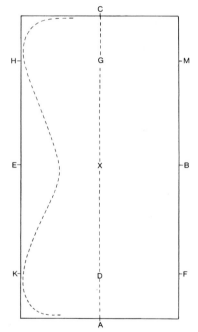

3 m loop in a 20 m × 40 m arena

COUNTER-CANTER

The Rider

The aids for counter-canter are the same as for the strike-off except that, just before you change from true canter to counter-canter, it may be advisable to draw the outside leg slightly further back. This is only to reinforce that aid to the horse so that he is not in a dilemma as to which leg he should be on. It also aids the control of the hindquarters and the bend.

During the movement the horse should remain curved to the leading leg. Your inside leg is chiefly responsible for keeping up the energy and the correct canter sequence. You will need an increasing degree of collection as movements become more demanding, so the horse may try to drop impulsion – in which case your inside leg will have to work harder.

There may be a temptation to hold the bend by too much use of the inside rein. It should be possible to give and re-take it without everything 'falling apart'. Try to discipline yourself to make this test quite often during your training. Control is reliant on the outside rein which, in conjunction with your other aids, should direct the movement and maintain speed and collection.

You may find problems occurring when you are beginning a new exercise. If the horse does not understand what you are asking, make it clearer by directing him with the appropriate rein even if this means that, for a moment, you lose the flexion to the leading leg. So long as you are holding him with firm seat and leg aids to keep him engaged, there should be no loss of balance. It will be important to keep your weight on the side of the leading leg the whole way through the movement. Any alteration may make the horse unbalanced and will be confusing when you come to the flying changes.

Counter-canter can feel very odd if you are not accustomed to it! Try to school yourself and the horse into it gradually by beginning with shallow loops. Sharp corners or sudden alterations of direction will almost certainly cause the horse to change legs or become disunited. If this happens, you should trot and start again.

Sharp corners or sudden alterations of direction will confuse the horse.

It is virtually impossible to ride counter-canter unless the horse is collected. In fact, if he is made to before his muscles are developed, it could do him harm. The smaller the arc you wish to ride, the more collection you need. Try to feel that you have the horse upright. By this I mean do not let him lean out, or less likely, lean in.

You are aiming for unity between yourself and the horse, so use your common sense. Do not be too ambitious. Prepare your canter carefully and, if you remind yourself constantly of the aids, you should not have too many problems.

REIN-BACK
The Judge

The FEI definition is:

1) The rein-back is an equilateral, retrograde movement in which the feet are raised and set down almost simultaneously by diagonal pairs. The feet should be well raised and the hind feet remain well in line.

2) At the preceding halt as well as during the rein-back the horse, although standing motionless and moving backwards respectively, should remain 'on the bit', maintaining his desire to move forward.

3) Anticipation or precipitation of the movement, resistance to or evasion of the hand, deviation of the quarters from the straight line, spreading or inactive hind legs and dragging forefeet are serious faults.

4) If in a dressage test a trot or canter is required after a rein-back, the horse should move off immediately into this pace, without a halt or an intermediate step.

You will first want to see a balanced halt, the hind legs being well under the hindquarters. The outline should be rounded, with the poll as the highest point.

When the horse steps back it is preferable that he picks up his feet, taking medium-size steps that are even to each other. Dragging steps or one or more steps being larger than the others are unsatisfactory. The sequence of steps should be as

227

near diagonal as possible. Crookedness or resistance should gain only a poor mark. It is also necessary to be strict about adherence to the number of steps specified in a particular test.

Sometimes the outline alters as the horse goes through the movement, or the size of steps may change. These faults should be penalised according to how they may affect the movement as a whole.

In this rein-back the horse has dropped his poll and is overbent.

REIN-BACK

The Trainer

Some novice horses can be quite stubborn about rein-back, refusing to take even one step. This is because they have not fully accepted a 'collecting aid', not wishing to engage their hindquarters and, at the same moment, yield in the mouth. The horse should be made compliant to these criteria. Also, before asking for rein-back, thorough work should be done on halts and transitions and shoulder-in to encourage suppleness. Shoulder-in will be invaluable for correcting crookedness. The half-halt is essential as a preparation for a satisfactory halt.

Try to make sure that pupils obtain a correct halt and help them to practise keeping the horse on the aids.

At first, when introducing rein-back, ask only for a step at a time, controlling the size of steps. If they become exaggerated, engagement and roundness are lost. Steps that are too small are generally so because the horse is resisting the aids. Dragging steps are a sign of stiffness in the joints and also show a reluctance to submit to the aids.

Riders may be tempted to pull the horse backwards. Getting them to use their legs in the right way will help them to discover the correct way to rein-back. The legs should be used to engage the hindquarters into the halt, kept in place while in halt to sustain it, and then used again gently to initiate the forward inclination prior to the first step back. Once this takes place, the legs should control the steps and the speed, being able to end the rein-back at any moment.

229

The hands should be able to maintain a pliable yield to the bit, which either asks the horse to go back, or allows him forward. The poll should remain as the highest point throughout the rein-back, but there should be no loss of roundness of the outline. The rider's weight may need to be adjusted to allow slight arching of the horse's back. This enables him to raise and put down his feet with height and deliberation.

The rein-back is a test of complete acceptance of hands and legs with a smooth response to the transitions, plus precision over the number and quality of steps.

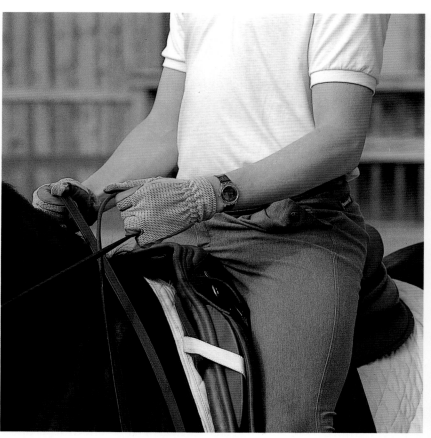

The hands should be able to maintain a pliable yield to the bit, asking him to go back, or allowing him to go forward.

REIN-BACK

The Rider

To ask the horse to rein-back, close your legs and ask him to step forward. Instead of allowing him to do so, gently restrain him, and ease the legs. If his mouth seems 'dull' or 'set', use an alternate action of the fingers until his jaw loosens and he yields to the pressure. Normally, finding that he cannot go forwards, he will then step back. After each step, a slight easing action may be used. The legs must control the straightness, the engagement, the size and number of steps.

Each diagonal step should feel deliberate, and even to the others. The back should feel slightly arched but not tense under your seat. It is important to keep the poll as the highest point throughout the movement. When you want to finish the steps, apply more pressure from the legs and allow forward movement with the hands. Try to feel for smoothness of transitions and avoid any rushing.

The sort of problems you may encounter are chiefly from stubbornness or anxiety. Stubborn horses can be difficult to persuade as they stand woodenly ignoring all aids! It may be helpful to teach this sort to rein-back from the ground, or with the help of a trainer who can tap the front legs with a schooling whip. Anxious horses are different altogether, needing a good deal of patience. Always try to establish a calm halt and only ask for a step at a time. Always go forwards if the horse becomes agitated. Never try to rein-back with the horse in a hollow outline, he cannot do what you want and may damage himself.

231

PIROUETTES IN WALK

The Judge

The FEI definition of pirouette work is as follows:

1) The pirouette (half-pirouette) is a circle (half-circle) executed on two tracks, with a radius equal to the length of the horse, the forehand moving round the haunches.

2) Pirouettes (half-pirouettes) are usually carried out at collected walk or canter, but can also be executed at piaffe.

3) At the pirouette (half-pirouette) the forefeet and the outside hind foot move round the inside hind foot, which forms the pivot and should return to the same spot or slightly in front of it, each time it leaves the ground.

4) At whatever pace the pirouettes (half-pirouettes) are executed, the horse, slightly bent to the direction in which he is turning, should remain 'on the bit' with a light contact, turn smoothly round, maintaining the exact cadence and sequence of footfalls of that pace. The poll stays the highest point during the entire movement.

5) During the pirouettes (half-pirouettes) the horse should maintain his impulsion, and never in the slightest way move backwards or deviate sideways. If the inside foot is not raised and returned to the ground in the same rhythm as the outside hind foot, the pace is no longer regular.

6) In executing the pirouette or the half pirouette in canter, the rider should maintain perfect lightness of the horse while accentuating the collection. The quarters are well engaged and lowered and show a good flexion of the joints.

7) The quality of the pirouettes (half-pirouettes) is judged according to the suppleness, lightness, cadence and regularity, and to the precision and smoothness of the transitions; pirouettes (half-pirouettes) at canter also according to the balance, the elevation and the number of strides (at pirouettes 6–8, at half-pirouettes 3–4 are desirable).

A good walk pirouette is only feasible if there is first a good collected walk. These are few and far between; many being false. The sort of faults you will see are loss of correct sequence, tension, breaks in gait or rhythm, steps of irregular size (uneven to each other), or 'creeping'.

Many riders 'cheat' by showing a half-halt but then continuing in a medium walk. Some do shorten the steps, but restrict the frame. In these cases this is often when the sequence is lost. Other riders simply go more slowly instead of more actively. When this happens the tempo, which altered from the medium walk, can cause the steps to 'stick' in the turn, through lack of energy. (This is the opposite of the ideal, which is that the tempo of steps during the turn should exactly match that of the preceding collected walk.)

In tests you will, generally, have to mark both pirouettes first, before giving the collected walk mark. This may seem confusing, but you will become accustomed to doing it this way, and be able to evaluate the walk in a corner of the mind, whilst also giving sufficient attention to the turns.

Many judges prefer to watch both pirouettes before giving marks. This is in order to compare them, so that if one is better than the other, the marks can be better differentiated. If you prefer, give the mark as the turn happens. In any case, your comment and mark must relate to each other. During the turn you should want to see the following: the maintenance of a correct rounded outline; the bend to the direction of the turn; activity of the steps throughout the turn; the hind feet remaining 'on the spot' or advancing minimally.

You will probably have to evaluate; loss of impulsion (some steps 'stuck'); loss of bend; hindquarters swinging out; too much advancement; unfinished turn; moving forward before the horse has returned to the line on which he started; stepping back; hollowing and resistance to the aids. Occasionally a horse will kick out to the rider's leg. You may also get a turn on the forehand or a turn on the centre. These last three faults should be penalised very severely. Pirouettes with some of the other faults should be valued according to the degree of the fault.

Right canter pirouette, but the horse appears to have lost impulsion and become overbent.

234

PIROUETTES IN WALK

The Trainer

For the FEI definition, see page 232. Pirouettes cannot be ridden satisfactorily without the ability to half-halt. This ties in with the other crucial issue, a good collected walk. You will have to make an assessment as to when the horse is ready to be collected with reference to his stage of training. Collecting too early, before the half-halt is established, will only cause problems such as resistance, tension and irregularities of gait.

'Training pirouettes' may be ridden earlier in the work, before this is achieved. These are turns, or segments of turns, made large on purpose, to give the horse a basic idea of the movement and the aids. They should be ridden with the correct bend, energy and outline. As training progresses, these turns are gradually brought smaller, with constant attention to the walk sequence and the submission. If the 'training pirouettes' are done properly, subsequent problems should be few. However, you may encounter some attempts at evasion, such as hindquarters stepping out, hollowing, loss of bend and so on. As with most problems, always 'return to base' – in this case, to a better collected walk.

Teaching pirouettes to the rider should be approached in the same manner as to the horse, i.e. a gradual build up, via a correct walk and 'training' turns, until a bend can be easily held, activity of steps maintained, and aids given in a co-ordinated way. From this beginning, it will be possible to reduce the size of the pirouette, bringing it gradually smaller, without losing any of the qualities needed to gain a good mark.

235

PIROUETTES IN WALK

The Rider

First of all you must learn to ride collected walk, because the steps in your turns should be in the same rhythm and tempo. (For advice on collection see page 178.)

It is most important that, in the approach to your pirouette, you do not feel any tension in the horse's back or his mouth, as this can obstruct the turn.

It will be a help if you take a shoulder-in position a few steps before the turn to prepare the horse. This position will place the shoulders ready and will give you the bend which should be maintained throughout the turn.

During the turn, your inside leg is responsible for the bend and for keeping the horse active, with forward inclination. If you fail to achieve this he may step back or 'stick' with one or both hind legs instead of stepping round.

The control of the collection is in the outside rein, used in conjunction with the other aids, and this may be employed for repeated half-halts to achieve a small enough turn. If this rein is ineffective, or allows the horse to bend his neck more than his body, the turn cannot work. With correct use of your outside rein and firm use of the outside leg, you should be able to control the hindquarters, which should never swing out. The feeling you should have is that, when you half-halt and put your outside leg on, the horse immediately moves away from it.

As you direct the horse round the turn with the inside rein, supported by the other aids, you may find that the horse is uncertain how to bring his forehand round unless he can move his quarters out. This can cause some difficulty until each aid has been understood. Try to be patient and take time. Also, when you start, do not expect to get the turns as small as they should be ultimately. Ride them much larger, with the accent on coming forwards and round little by little.

Throughout all pirouettes try to give your attention to the correctness of the outline. If you fail in this respect you will make it far too awkward for the horse, and may cause him to resist unnecessarily.

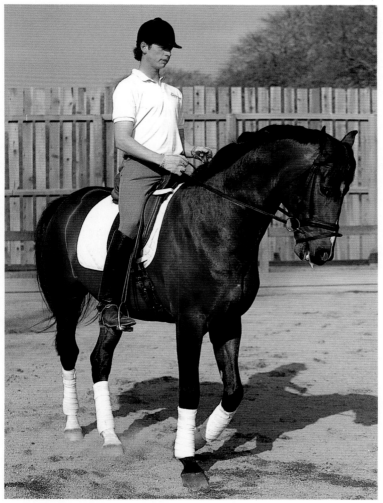

Be patient and take your time; do not make it awkward for the horse.

CANTER PIROUETTES

The Judge

The FEI definitions of pirouette work are listed on page 232 (Pirouettes in Walk). As a canter pirouette calls for a lowering of the hindquarters with the horse supporting his weight on his hind legs, it is obviously important that he shows excellent collection and acceptance of the aids. Any flaws will cause him to resist or try to evade the strain put on his joints.

Pirouettes seldom match each other. The horse may find one direction easier, and the rider is very often co-ordinated better to one side than the other. There will be many faults to assess and it may be hard to evaluate them for marks. Some of the common faults are:

Too big. Many turns are too large and are more like 'training pirouettes', used at home when teaching the horse the movement. However, in your evaluation bear in mind that a large pirouette can generally be brought smaller (so long as the gait is correct) and is less likely to strain the horse, so a certain amount of leniency could be shown.

'Rearing' round. A bad fault, in my opinion, as the canter has lost forward momentum and the horse is no longer in a rounded outline. He has also 'come off the aids'. This sort of turn would be extremely detrimental to future work.

Stepping back. Also a bad fault as impulsion has obviously died; the horse has almost certainly hollowed and he is unbalanced.

Canter pirouette left – Carl Hester on Giorgione

Unbalanced or rushed. The horse may try to swing round without keeping a correct canter stride. It cannot be categorically stated how many strides it should take to complete a turn, but you could base your assessment on approximately four for a half-pirouette and eight for a full turn. If the strides do not match each other in width or size the collection and balance may be at fault.

Changing leg. Lack of balance or bend can cause this to happen, or it may be an evasion of the aids. Either way, it can cause serious problems. The horse may well become upset or worried as he finds himself in difficulty.

Losing bend. This is mainly a rider error as, if the horse were kept correctly on the aids, it would be unlikely to occur.

Hollowing. If this happens it should be viewed seriously as, in addition to affecting his training, it can be very harmful to the horse physically.

Breaks in the gait. Chiefly a rider fault as, if the impulsion is not being maintained, the horse is likely to break because of the difficulty of the movement.

Hindquarters swinging out. You will often see this happen, and it does so because the rider fails to take a shoulder-in position in the approach. The horse will be at a big disadvantage as his forehand gets left behind in the turn. It may well cause other problems because the horse is hampered in several respects.

Stepping together behind. When momentum, balance or round-ness of outline are mislaid, some horses save themselves by turning in a series of 'bunny hops'. This is obviously a bad fault as the canter gait is impaired.

Not completed. This is simply when a turn is not finished properly and ends up on a different line from the approach. It is not a very bad fault but certainly one which must be taken into account, especially at the higher levels.

CANTER PIROUETTES

The Trainer

Successful production of canter pirouettes will depend entirely on the canter itself. If it is correct, that is, in correct sequence, showing a moment of suspension, and straight, the right basis is present. There must also be good submission to collection and the half-halt aids.

In the approach, a shoulder-in position should be taken as a preparation and the half-halts continued into, and during the turn.

When teaching either horse or rider, ask for only a couple of steps of the turn to start with. This should enable the rider to find out how to use the inside leg to retain impulsion and how to use the outside rein to control the gait and the turn. The rider will also need to discover how to control the hindquarters with the outside leg and how much flexion to take with the inside rein.

You may find that a useful lead up to these turns is to put the horse in a travers position on a circle and then reduce the size. If anything starts to go wrong it is then fairly simple to make the rider go forwards onto a larger circle in order to repair any mistakes. Only when you can see that both parties have grasped the exercises in principle should you allow the rider to attempt to reduce the size of the circle.

If the horse should make a four-beat canter, drop impulsion and lift his forehand to get round, or if he should resist the aids or change leg, you should take it as a warning that all is not right and review the situation.

241

Some horses will pirouette well on one rein and not so well on the other. This may result from the rider's co-ordination being better one way, or it could be that insufficient attention has been given to suppleness or acceptance of the aids.

Left canter pirouette showing good engagement of the hindquarters.

CANTER PIROUETTES

The Rider

Although canter pirouettes are great fun to ride, you can easily get into an awful muddle. Therefore, first make sure that you are thoroughly clear about the aids and have practised many pirouettes in walk, so that you understand about preparation and the use of the aids during the turn.

Canter pirouettes are great fun to ride.

243

It is crucial that your canter is sufficiently collected and that you can achieve and maintain good collection by means of half-halts. (It is a good idea to practise this on a circle before you ever think of a pirouette.)

It may be useful to prepare for your turns by riding travers on a circle of approximately 10 m, alternating this with shoulder-in position. This should help you to get control and learn to keep the gait true. A shoulder-in position in the approach will give you the best chance for a successful turn, provided that the horse is attending to the aids.

Just as in walk, the canter pirouette should start large, with only a few steps asked for, before riding forwards into an active canter on a larger circle. From this base you can gradually reduce the size and/or increase the number of steps.

It is most important to keep the canter correct; to make sure that the horse is rounded and that a bend is maintained. Your aids should reflect this. Also, control of the width of each step is vital if balance is to be maintained. If you find that you strike resistance or the horse breaks the gait, do ride forwards immediately and prepare again.

Most problems occur because the horse has found a loophole somewhere to escape or avoid such a demanding exercise. It is up to you to use the aids effectively and ensure that this does not happen.

FLYING CHANGES

The Judge

The FEI definition is:

> This change of leg is executed in close connection with the suspension which follows each stride of canter. Flying changes of leg can also be executed in series, for instance at every 4th, 3rd, 2nd or at every stride. The horse, even in the series, remaining light, calm and straight with lively impulsion, maintaining the same rhythm and balance throughout the series concerned. In order not to restrict or restrain the lightness and fluency of the flying changes of leg in series, the degree of collection should be slightly less than otherwise at collected canter.

There are quite a lot of people who have difficulty in seeing whether a change is true or not. If you are one of these I am afraid you should not accept judging appointments at this level! At the lower stages of training you should be quick to recognise which leg a horse is on or when he is disunited. In fact you should be able to see which leg he is going to strike off with even before he does it! It is also necessary to be quick enough to see, if he becomes disunited, whether he changed in front or behind. Sometimes it happens in one stride but you must be able to pick this up. All this preparation should help in developing the sort of close observation needed to see changes.

Most changes that go wrong in the arena are 'late behind' – that is to say the hind leg does not follow through at precisely

245

Flying change – Carl Hester on Giorgione

the same moment as the foreleg. Very occasionally you might see one 'late in front'. Usually the horse corrects himself a half or one stride later. Uncorrected, it would become a disunited canter. There are also changes that are 'short behind', or 'not through'. These are true changes but ones in which the horse has taken a short step with the inside hind leg in the moment of the change. The cause of these could be lack of impulsion, a poor response to the leg aids or a resistance, possibly in the mouth.

Many incorrect changes occur because the moment of suspension is insufficient. In other words, there is not actually time for the horse to change properly – usually because of lack of impulsion, engagement or balance. Changes that swing from one side to the other, are performed almost 'on the spot', or 'dwell', are caused by the horse not going forward.

Changes which, although perhaps 'mechanically' correct, are full of tension and resistance are examples of poor training. Those that are ridden with insufficient collection should also be penalised.

In the 'tempi' changes, mistakes will occur. If the quality has been good before and after, one mistake should not be classed as insufficient. If, on the other hand, there were already some faults plus one or more mistake, this would be counted as insufficient.

Flying changes should ideally match the canter – although a slightly more expressive stride is certainly acceptable, or even desirable.

The rider should have an established position which should be maintained through the changes. Quite often a rider is seen to swing the body, or twist, in order to get the change. This should be noted in the rider mark as it detracts from the classical picture and can also be detrimental to the horse's balance and ability to stay straight.

Excessive swinging of the legs is also unattractive and should not be necessary if the horse has been trained correctly. Leaning forwards inevitably brings the seat out of the saddle where it is then not in a position to engage the horse's hindquarters. Any restriction by the reins or swinging the horse's head from side to side is a hindrance to the horse and may cause resistance. All aids should be unobtrusive.

FLYING CHANGES

The Trainer

Teaching the horse to do flying changes can be a matter of extreme delicacy – although some horses take to them 'like a duck to water'. Temperament is the key factor and those who are 'laid back' do not generally get worked up – in fact aids often need to be backed up by the schooling whip.

Any horse who becomes agitated easily is a prime subject for finding changes impossibly exciting. Such horses can be very awkward to train, taking longer than their less excitable counterparts. Changes tend to 'blow their minds', so a lot of preparation has to take place. This usually involves really establishing all the canter work to obtain calmness and obedience before any attempt can be made. Even then, the execution of just a single change can cause havoc! Only by patient persistence and preventing any anticipation will there be a chance of overcoming the problem. Once a single change has been accepted, it may be some time before any 'tempi' changes should be attempted. It is often a case of trying some then forgetting them for a while. As the horse's obedience becomes more established in his general work, it all becomes more possible.

Calmer horses are much easier. They may show little response to a given aid but, with some help from the whip, will usually effect a change. If they are lazy they might be 'late behind' or 'short behind' but this can be rectified relatively easily by improved activity and impulsion.

Changes tend to blow their minds ...

Once this type has understood the aids, it becomes comparatively simple to establish a simple change, and fairly soon you could lead into the 'tempi' changes. Achieving straightness in these is sometimes troublesome. Keeping up engagement with the horse well 'forward to the hands' in a rounded outline is the right approach. Even the most recalcitrant can be brought to this state with sufficient determination.

It is exceedingly demanding to have to teach this exercise to rider and horse if they are both new to it. It is far simpler first to teach the rider on a trained horse the feel of the aids and when to ask. However, if this is not possible, you may perhaps tackle the problem the other way round and give the horse the idea yourself, then put the two together. At any rate, your knowledge of how to obtain changes and of the best place to ask for them, and your ability to help the rider from the ground will be crucial.

FLYING CHANGES

The Rider

Tackling this exercise can sometimes be rather baffling as, on one day the horse can appear completely confident, while on another he has apparently never heard of it!

There are three main points to work on before you should even ask for changes:

1) The canter must be correct, with a clear moment of suspension.

2) The horse must be obedient of the strike-off aids.

3) The horse should be able to perform simple changes with one stride of walk.

This preparation should lay the foundations from which it is possible for the horse to change: the next step is to help him understand what you want. Clearly, you must first be certain that you know how you are going to ask him. This should be apparent if your aids are one hundred per cent successful. Although the position you put the horse in is far more important than where you attempt the change, there are certain places which can aid your efforts. For example, the end of a diagonal, or following a 10 m half-circle and return to the track, or at the end of a half-pass. There are many other options, but the important things to remind yourself of are to have the balance right and to have the horse 'on the aids'. It is very easy to change legs by altering the balance and catching the horse off guard, but this is a deception which will only delay the correct response.

When you ask for your first flying change you will hopefully set it up right and use familiar aids. However, reinforcing the aids with a little help from the whip may be useful so long as the horse does not become worried. If you have enough impulsion and you remember to change the bend, maintain a good position and use your aids effectively, you may be fortunate enough to achieve your change straight away. Reward the horse, and put him back in the stable. When he comes out again the next day he should remember. Gradually, you can build on this.

It may be as well to settle for a change in only one direction to start with, as trying to go both ways may at first be confusing. If your horse becomes sulky — which some do — try to make the work as easy as you can and keep him going well forwards. He may need a few reprimands, but keep him cheerful with a pat on the neck when he has done well.

Excitable horses are the most difficult. Very thorough preparation and a lot of patience are necessary. Whenever the changes cause too much agitation you have to regain obedience and calmness before you try again. If the horse will really accept being collected and will remain in a rounded outline, you should win through eventually, but it could take time.

Sometimes it is not easy to feel when changes are correct. A horse may not always change true, but leave one foot behind — which may or may not follow later. If it does not, you should recognise that he is disunited, in which case it is best to stop, and start again. When you are practising, it is most helpful to have an assistant or trainer on the ground to let you know if a change is correct. This saves many mistakes being made, either from the horse or on your part.

'Tempi' changes are a matter of gradual development. Only when the horse is well established in a single change should you consider a sequence. Even then, it is wise to put two together in the sequence you want, and then three and so on. This way you can keep a constant check on the canter itself; on the straightness and balance, the roundness and acceptance of the aids. It also gives you time to ensure that you are sitting correctly and applying the aids efficiently.

COUNTER-CHANGES OF HAND

The Judge

The FEI definition is:

> When changing direction in form of counter-change of hand, the rider changes direction by moving obliquely either to the quarter line or the centre line or to the opposite long side of the arena, whence he returns on an oblique line to the line he was following when he started the movement.
>
> At the counter-change of hand the rider should make his horse straight an instant before changing direction.
>
> When, for instance, at counter-change of hand at half-pass to either side of the centre line, the number of metres or strides to either side is prescribed in the test, it must be strictly observed and the movement be executed symmetrically.

In tests, all counter-changes of hand are specified either by distance or by strides. For example, in trot it may be ridden from quarter marker to X, change of bend and X to quarter marker (on the same long side). Alternatively, it can be ridden as a zigzag on either side of the centre line, for example 3 m, 6 m, 6 m, 3 m. With the latter, the rider should achieve an equal number of steps in each of the 3 m distances and similarly in the 6 m. If this is not the case, it may show a lack of suppleness. In all counter-changes of hand, the horse should show an equal amount of bend to each direction.

In canter zigzags there should of course be a correct flying change at each change of direction.

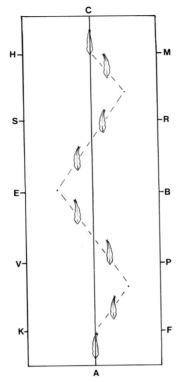

Counter-change of hand (zigzag)

Some common faults are:

Anticipation of change of lead in canter. If the horse becomes used to a zigzag he will learn that there will be changes of lead. As the rider prepares on the straight stride (the final one prior to a new direction) the horse may well change then. Clearly, this is a disobedience. If there was a lot of anticipation, it should be reflected in the submission mark at the end of the test.

Late answering the aid. Although less frequent than anticipation, this is by no means rare. It will result in a muddle, as the rider wishes to proceed in the new direction but, for a stride, is on the wrong leg. The horse *may* be corrected calmly but, more likely, there will be resistance, loss of balance and so on. The mark would depend on how soon a recovery was made.

253

Canter: one-time changes – Carl Hester on Giorgione

Lack of collection and engagement. The horse will labour through the movement and will be unlikely to fit in the specified steps or strides. This fault is serious as, uncorrected, it will impede any improvement.

Lack of impulsion. Without sufficient impulsion the gait cannot be sustained and may break. None of the work can be of much value without adequate energy.

Lack of bend/too much bend in the neck. As the bend is relative to the angle of each half-pass, this can only be assessed knowing what that angle is. However, the curve of the horse should be uniform from nose to tail and not show more bend in the neck than in the body. Any lack of bend may illuminate a stiffness which is opposed to basic principles in general, and to this exercise in particular. It will generally cause an awkwardness in the movement and, additionally, may bring about uneven steps or strides, or lack of rhythm.

Unlevelness or alteration of tempo. Unlevel steps are a fundamental fault, to be viewed seriously. Changes in tempo are also unsat-isfactory but are less serious than unlevelness. Most unlevelness results from stiffness through the horse or may be to do with the mouth. Any uneven acceptance of the bit can cause unlevel steps. This will be particularly obvious in this exercise as will an uneven bend with one side showing more than the other. If you notice resistance to the bit in the change of bend, or more bend one way, the movement will inevitably be marked down, but a comment made to the rider at the end may be helpful as it is of the utmost importance to future work that this is corrected.

Hindquarters leading or trailing. Trailing quarters could result from lack of response to the rider's outside leg, or be caused by stiffness. Quarters leading can be an overreaction to the outside leg or, more likely, the rider has failed to position the forehand properly. You may have to make a decision about the root cause. If the rider is chiefly at fault, this should be taken into account in the rider mark at the end of the test.

Incorrect number of steps. This should be evaluated in the same way as any inaccuracy or lack of precision, and the severity of the penalty should depend on the level of the test. As well as making a calculation about the accuracy of the number of steps you should also take into account the distance that the horse covers. If engagement and impulsion are correct, the moment of suspension will provide the gait with a chance to 'cover ground'; if these are lacking the horse will be able to travel less far. The rider should be in a position to re-direct the horse and to change the bend without causing resistance or upsetting the regularity and flow of the gait. Any restriction or false collection should be apparent by the lack of ease of the movement. Running out of space is another hazard for the rider but if the horse is properly collected this should not be a problem.

COUNTER-CHANGES OF HAND

The Trainer

IN TROT

Following the development of the half-pass, the horse and rider should now be ready to tackle a counter-change of hand in trot on both reins. Make sure that the change of bend has plenty of space to start with and that the rider takes time to make the changeover. At first, the horse should be allowed to straighten and the forehand should be taken into the new position before the bend is taken up and the horse asked to go in the new direction.

Any resistance or difficulty should be ironed out by allowing the horse to move forwards, and better engagement and collection should be established. Irregular steps should be eradicated immediately by checking up on submission to the aids and also by returning to shoulder-in. Although the neck should be pliable, with no tension in the poll, do not allow too much bend to be taken in the neck as this could inhibit success.

The horse should be upright; he should not be allowed to lean in, or fall onto his outside shoulder. Control of his hindquarters should be achieved from the use of shoulder-in, and they should never be allowed to lead or trail.

IN CANTER

In canter the same qualities should apply but of course a flying change is also part of the movement. Obviously a counter-

Any resistance should be ironed out.

change of hand should not be attempted unless the horse has fully understood and accepted a simple flying change to each direction. As with the trot, a horse new to the exercise will need time to make the changeover. A straight stride should be taken for the flying change and then the forehand positioned for the new direction. The number of steps or strides should not necessarily be taken into account at first. The quality of the lateral work and the change is more important − putting it all together with greater accuracy can come later.

When your pupil reaches this stage, the last stride of the preceding direction should be ridden forwards and used for the change and the re-positioning. The bend is then present in the first stride of the next direction.

In tests, a specified distance or number of strides is required, so this must be attended to, as well as making sure that it can all be fitted into the required distance.

COUNTER-CHANGES OF HAND

The Rider

All the principles of half-pass apply, so all you have to worry about is the changeover or, in the case of zigzags, fitting it into the distance given!

IN TROT

If, for example, you are riding a half-pass to the right and you wish to change this to travel left, you should be aware of the time needed for the horse to accomplish his change of bend. He cannot be expected to do this in two steps when he is first learning – although this might be the aim later.

Make sure that you take a shoulder-in position for your new direction, and that your outside leg holds the hindquarters in place and does not allow them to lead. You should feel that the weight is taken evenly by the horse's shoulders as, should he lean in or fall out, the change of bend will be difficult. Also, you must try to show equality of bend and steps in each direction and only allow as much width of stride as your particular horse can cope with. Keep up the impulsion and collection as this will enable you to cover distance in the moment of suspension.

If you feel any unlevelness or difficulty in keeping the rhythm, or if the horse struggles in any way, do pause for thought and possibly reorganise. This might mean going back to walk temporarily to sort out the problem.

IN CANTER

First and foremost, the correct sequence of the canter is your main concern.

You should have thoroughly established a single flying change, which the horse can perform without excitement or anticipation. At the start, when you come to the changeover, ride forwards first, and get the change before you try to go the other way. As time goes on, you should be able to marry your change to the new bend by riding one bend followed by a forward change stride, then the other bend. In each direction a shoulder-in position should be used as a preparation.

Do not expect the horse instantly to have control over himself in these exercises. He may well lose his balance or get muddled. Clear aids, good preparation and patience should take you in the right direction. If you meet any resistances, or the horse becomes excitable, always try to make the exercise simpler again and then come back to it.

He may well get muddled.

PIAFFE

The Judge

The FEI definition is:

1) The piaffe is a highly measured, collected, cadenced, elevated and majestic trot on the spot. The horse's back is supple and vibrating. The quarters are slightly lowered, the haunches with active hocks are well engaged, giving great freedom, lightness and mobility to the shoulders and forehand. Each diagonal pair of feet is raised and returned to the ground alternately, with an even cadence and a slightly prolonged suspension.

2) In principle, the height of the toe of the raised foreleg should be level with the middle of the cannon bone of the other foreleg. The toe of the raised hind leg should reach just above the fetlock joint of the other hind leg.

3) The neck should be raised and arched, the head vertical. The horse should remain light 'on the bit' with a supple poll, maintaining a light soft contact on a taut rein. The body of the horse should move up and down in a supple, cadenced and harmonious movement.

4) The piaffe, although being executed strictly on the spot and with perfect balance, must always be animated by a lively impulsion, which is displayed in the horse's constant desire to move forward as soon as the aids calling for the piaffe cease.

5) Moving even slightly backwards, irregular steps with the hind legs, crossing the forelegs or swinging either the forehand or the quarters from one side to the other are serious faults. A movement with hurried and unlevel or irregular steps without cadence, or steps without suspension cannot be called a true piaffe.

Piaffe — Ferdi Eilberg on Demonstrator

The chief problem in judging this movement is the very brief time you have to make the assessment. In the Grand Prix, it is connected to passage, with marks for both, plus the transitions, so time is short.

If you are judging at this level, you will have studied the movement so will be able to determine what is a good piaffe. You will be aware of the importance of lowered hindquarters, because this degree of engagement, giving the forehand its capacity to lift, is what the process of training is all about. It cannot take place without roundness of outline, suppleness and complete obedience. Nor can diagonal steps, rhythm and regularity be obtained unless the basis, the trot itself, is correct.

261

You will have studied a good piaffe.

Height is dependent on the degree of energy (impulsion) that is put into it, and this is dependent upon perfect balance.

If in doubt as to what mark to give, search your knowledge of the fundamental issues of training.

PIAFFE

The Trainer

For the FEI definition see page 260. You may train the horse for this exercise in two ways. You can be mounted and teach him from on top, or put him in a cavesson with a lunge rein and teach him from the ground.

TEACHING PIAFFE MOUNTED

If you prefer the first method you should initially ensure that the half-halt is established. Without this, you will not be able to obtain the necessary engagement and collection. The horse should be established in his trot gait, being regular and rhythmic. He must also be straight and willingly accept the collecting aids.

As a preliminary exercise you may teach him to simply shorten his steps for a few strides and then go forwards. Some trainers prefer to walk into piaffe steps to begin with and trot out of them. This can help to encourage engagement in the early stages and both horse and pupil may find it easier.

As there will be many evasions to this exercise you will have to use your expertise to teach both parties to overcome any sticky moments. Generally speaking, any troublesome situations are best dealt with by returning to basics.

If you are teaching the horse yourself from the saddle or are helping pupils, it is most necessary to be able to use a schooling whip to reinforce leg aids. It may be simpler to obtain a result

263

from the ground but at the end of the day, riders must be able to produce the steps themselves.

So often in the arena the piaffe fails, the rider being unable to get a response. This can happen in any case, but as a trainer you must do your best to ensure that the horse is taught the aids properly, that he fully understands them and that the rider can obtain a response without your help. As with any new exercise, time is of the essence but expectation of success should come from the knowledge that the build-up has been thorough.

TEACHING PIAFFE FROM THE GROUND

If you believe in teaching this exercise from the ground, you will need the horse in tack with a lungeing cavesson over a snaffle bridle and side reins from the bit to the girth. The horse should be accustomed to being lunged and must not be in any way frightened of a whip. You will need to stand by the head facing the tail, in a position where you can control the amount of 'going forwards', and use the whip on the hind leg, just above the hock. If you stand next to a wall, hedge, or fence you will be able to obtain the effect from the whip without the horse swinging his quarters out.

When the horse feels the whip he should flex the leg, putting it under his body, thus lowering the hindquarters. If the whip is used in the rhythm you want (as for very collected trot), and the lunge rein is used as you would the reins for half-halt, the horse should produce the steps you are looking for. Because you can see exactly what is happening, being on the ground does have an advantage. Once the horse understands, you can introduce the rider and the aids that he will be using while still in your control. Both horse and rider will get the feel of what is wanted in this way.

As the lowering of the hindquarters is so crucial to the correct quality of this exercise, do make sure that the preparation for it is thorough. Some horses will have natural ability for piaffe; others will not. When choosing a horse for top class dressage, it is worth seeing his reaction to a few shorter steps (in walk will do). Some do have great difficulty which, of course, will present a big handicap later on.

PIAFFE

The Rider

Although piaffe is not required in tests until Intermediare Level, it will be introduced much earlier in training. The value of this is to teach the horse to put his hindquarters underneath him, and to be more active. It is used initially when you are teaching the horse to become more engaged, but the steps will be ridden slightly forwards, not on the spot, as in Grand Prix.

The preparation for this exercise is the half-halt, for without it you will not be able to collect enough to obtain shorter steps. By using a series of half-halts it will be possible to reduce the size of the steps which, if then activated, will become piaffe. It is important to keep the horse straight and impulsive.

The feel of piaffe will be similar to a soft bounce underneath you. If it feels 'flat', quick, or shuffling it will not be right. The rhythm should be the same as the trot work. It is crucial that the rhythm is exact and that the sequence of steps is diagonal, as for trot.

When you start to teach your horse to do this, you may begin from a collected walk, making a transition into a very collected trot, then returning to walk. This way both of you have time to make adjustments to balance, the degree of collection, response to aids and so on. At all times you should feel that if you give a forward aid, the horse will respond. Your contact with the mouth should be such that, from a slight use of the fingers, you can half-halt or, by an easing, allow the horse forward. The horse must not on any account 'drop the

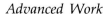

bit' or come 'above' or 'behind' it. Stepping back is a serious fault as it means you have allowed the horse to come 'off the aids'.

Control over the number of steps is important. To begin with you should ask only for two or three, developing the number only once the horse has thoroughly understood the aids and will remain straight, submissive and calm.

Although repetition is necessary to comprehension, be careful not to overdo the exercise. Once the horse has learnt about it he may use it as an evasion to going forwards, or in anticipation when in walk. The latter can spoil your walk work if he continually breaks the rhythm.

Later on, when you have reached a higher stage of training, you will need to regulate the number of steps precisely. If your preparation is done diligently and entails the horse's complete understanding and acceptance of control, the ultimate work will present fewer hitches.

Do not become over-reliant on your trainer.

Although you will have needed assistance from your trainer in practice, do be careful that you are not *reliant* upon his help from the ground. Your horse should learn to answer the aids as for any other exercise. All to often you will find yourself 'at a loss' in the arena, if you do not confirm the answer you want on your own.

PASSAGE

The Judge

The FEI definition is:

1) This is a measured, very collected, very elevated and very cadenced trot. It is characterised by a pronounced engagement of the quarters, a more accentuated flexion of the knees and hocks, and the graceful elasticity of the movement. Each diagonal pair of feet is raised and returned to the ground alternately, with cadence and a prolonged suspension.

2) In principle, the height of the toe of the raised foreleg should be level with the middle of the cannon bone of the other foreleg. The toe of the raised hind leg should be slightly above the fetlock joint of the other hind leg.

3) The neck should be raised and gracefully arched with the poll as the highest point and the head close to the vertical. The horse should remain light and soft 'on the bit' and be able to go smoothly from the passage to the piaffe and vice-versa, without apparent effort and without altering the cadence, the impulsion being always lively and pronounced.

4) Irregular steps with the hind legs, swinging the forehand or the quarters from one side to the other as jerky movements of the forelegs or the hind legs or dragging the hind legs are serious faults.

267

Passage — Ferdi Eilberg on Arun Tor

Because this movement is the culmination of the horse's training in trot, much will depend on how that has been done. You are bound to see some defects and making a valuation of them can be hard. There are several faults that come to mind:

Low passage. This is when the height of the steps is less than in the definition of the movement. In some cases it is little more than an elevated trot, lacking flexibility in the joints of the hindquarters and also lacking any lowering of the croup.

Although it may maintain a steady rhythm, it could never be considered worth a good mark.

Irregular passage. Quite often you will find that one hind leg may flex more than the other, or it will step further under than the other. Also one foreleg may come higher than the other, or one may take a shorter or longer step. In any of these instances the gait is impaired and should be marked down accordingly, particularly if it is persistently incorrect. As with any irregularity the cause is probably lack of suppleness and/or resistance on one side of the horse's mouth and is a serious fault.

Loss of rhythm and/or height. There will be occasions when, although the steps are basically satisfactory, momentary alteration in the rhythm and possibly the height is seen. This is not, in itself, a serious fault but it probably indicates a loss of impulsion. If it is repaired quickly, and the quality of the steps before and after is correct, a moderate mark could be given. If it only occurred briefly during a sequence this would not be unacceptable, but more frequent occurrence would clearly be more serious.

Dragging hind feet. This, in my view, is a particularly unattractive manifestation of passage and opposed to all the fundamental qualities of training. It means to me that the hindquarters are not engaged under the horse and that the back is tense, and not rounded. Often it results from false collection where the rider has drawn in the head and neck leaving the hindquarters trailing. In some cases the true sequence of the gait is lost with the hind legs almost walking! The rider may be obliged to show considerable movement of the body in order to absorb the horse's action but this should be expressed through suppleness rather than any looseness of the seat or inability to hold position. Snatching of the hands in an upward motion or excessive flapping of the legs may be mentioned in the rider mark but only if it has affected the performance. Some riders manage to break the rules successfully!

PASSAGE

The Trainer

For the FEI definition see page 267. If all the basic work has been developed in the right way, the trot should now be at a stage where the balance, impulsion and collection permit the final stage to be started. Acceptance of the half-halt should be as near perfect as possible, and the horse should be making no objection to taking the pressures put upon him.

The collected steps should be established in an exact rhythm, with no irregularities. They may now be brought into a more cadenced form by the increase of impulsion combined with the half-halt. When the horse understands and accepts this, more height can evolve gradually – at first for only a step or two but, as time goes on, the movement can be sustained over a longer distance.

The horse will need much assistance in retaining balance and in sustaining the necessary lowering of the hindquarters to carry his weight.

You can be of help to the rider, from the ground, with the aid of a schooling whip to give rhythm and keep up energy, but in the arena the rider cannot have this assistance, so you should make sure that aids are being answered.

When teaching this exercise do remember that it is very strenuous for the horse. To avoid strain it should be developed gradually, in small doses. The rider, who will also have to put in a lot of effort and concentration, should not be overtaxed either.

Horses who have a good natural moment of suspension will

certainly find this movement easier than those who do not. The latter will find it awkward to produce and may never give adequate height, even if they achieve the rhythm. Temperament will also play its part, as the very idle may never give the movement the vibrance it should show, whereas the anxious horse may become far too tense under the pressures involved.

TRANSITIONS BETWEEN PASSAGE AND PIAFFE

The principles of all transitions are the same but, because of the control needed to move from passage to piaffe (or vice versa), the use of the half-halt, refined to its highest degree, is essential to the achievement of fluency. A gradual reduction (or increase, as appropriate) in the size of steps, whilst maintaining balance, impulsion and lightness, is the key to good transitions between these two movements. Good feel is needed on the part of the pupil to know the degree of half-halt to use and when. A schoolmaster can perhaps introduce the rider to this feel best but your expertise will be relied on a good deal. You should be able to ride the horse 'from the ground' if you are to help you pupil satisfactorily. Any loss of impulsion or collection should be corrected at once. If the horse becomes anxious or resistant, make the pupil ride forwards immediately. Determining the length of time to practise depends on the mental and physical ability of both horse and rider but although progress must be made, beware of overdoing it. Fatigue by either party will only result in deterioration rather than improvement.

In dressage, there are, inevitably, a few horses who show a serious lack of ability for a particular exercise. Passage, which demands the highest degree of collection, is a prime example. When this situation arises, it has, unfortunately, to be accepted. It is very disappointing but, if it happens, that horse may have to be discarded for one with more aptitude. Sadly, you may have to be the one to inform the owner of the horse of any real stumbling blocks. Then, depending on their ambition, they can decide for themselves whether or not to keep him.

PASSAGE

The Rider

To reach this culmination of the work in trot is exciting, but also demanding. You should therefore have built a very sound base upon which to conclude your work in this gait.

Gradually, throughout your training, you will have taught the horse a greater degree of collection. From this he will have learned to accept the aids and be in a position to carry himself with lowered hindquarters. He will understand about activity and be able to produce more impulsion without losing balance. He will understand the half-halt, the use of which is essential to achieving passage.

You should, at all times, be able to produce and maintain an exact rhythm in a regular stride (even steps).

All the suppling work you should have done will have prepared the horse physically, so there should be no tense or stiff muscles to inhibit freedom or flexibility. Mentally, he should have become your partner, fully understanding, confident and co-operative, happy to try to answer whatever new question is asked of him.

When you wish to attempt some passage steps you will have to build your impulsion, together with the half-halt. Feeling the restraint, the horse should spring more, giving you height. Your leg aids should coincide with the rhythm you are searching for, and, combined with the half-halt aids, will gradually give the required 'feel'. Some horses will have a great deal of spring but, if a horse is supple in his back, he will not throw you out of the saddle. In any case, your position should by

The rider needs to acquire a feel for elevation.

now be extremely secure.

At first only a few steps should be asked for – even one is a start! Try to be appreciative and give a reward, by your voice, or by a pat on the neck. As with all work, understanding is sometimes slow, but careful, patient perseverance will prevail. If you become frustrated, you will only cause yourself more problems and you could spoil everything. A calm but determined approach is needed.

Horses who do not have much elevation in their trot can be a problem, as judges do not really want to see a low passage which is scarcely more than an elevated trot. All you can do in such cases is make sure you demand as much impulsion as possible.

Even if it takes some of them longer than others, most horses can be persuaded to perform most Grand Prix movements but, occasionally, one will have little or no aptitude for a particular movement – passage being a prime example. If this should happen, I must advise that you give serious consideration as to whether it is worth pursuing your objective. If there is some real drawback it can only result in awful frustration, which is no good to anyone.

EXIT

Exit

THE JUDGE

Every test requires that the competitor leaves the arena at A on a long rein; this is still part of the test. As such, consideration should be given to any untoward occurrence. Although most competitors will know the rules and do the right thing, it will be up to you to make a decision as to how important a discrepancy may be, and make your judgement accordingly.

THE TRAINER

At the end of a test, after the immobility, the rider should walk on a long rein to A. Your responsibility is to make sure that they know this and that they realise that it is still part of the test.

They may turn right or left at C and do not have to follow the track, but may take a direct line to A.

THE RIDER

After the immobility at the end of the test, you may ease the reins and pat the horse. Do remember to finish the immobility properly, not allowing any anticipation. You can turn whichever way you want at C (usually right) and then head for A. The horse should walk out calmly, stretching his head and neck downward.

However excited or fed up you may be, don't forget that this is still part of the test and could be judged!

The relief when it's over!

Conclusion

It is often difficult for judges, trainers and riders to 'come together' over the various issues involved in competition dressage, as each has their own individual problems and priorities. However, I think it is important to remember that all three have need of each other in the general scheme of things, and that there would be no competitions otherwise.

It is easy for anyone to become isolated in their own section, putting blame for lack of success on someone else. All will benefit from having an open mind, referring constantly to others who have reached world class status.

Sometimes I think that, in the endeavours of humans to attain their goals, the horses are forgotten. Their feelings and welfare should not be neglected by ignorant or unsympathetic riding. It is sickening to see natural beauty or spirit destroyed through insensitivity.

Everyone who rides, trains or judges should encourage peaceful co-operation, giving due respect to each other and in particular, to the horse.